Never Far from Dancing

A series of interviews with some of ⌐   ⌐most dancers in twentieth-century ballet, *Never Far from Dancing* reflects on the paths that their careers have taken since they retired from the stage. Barbara Newman has expertly edited each of her interviews to read as a monologue, addressing every aspect of ballet, from its styles and technical demands to its personalities, its celebrated roles and, most of all, what happens when the dancing stops.

While ballet invites all manner of writing from critics, admirers and academics, the thoughts and experiences of the dancers themselves are seldom recorded. Here, those who scaled the heights of their art hand down their wisdom and recount lives spent in this most enduring of art forms.

Barbara Newman has written extensively on dance for *Dance Magazine* (USA), the *Dancing Times* (UK) and many other periodicals and major reference works. She has written numerous books on ballet, including *Striking a Balance* (1982), *Grace under Pressure* (2003), and *The Illustrated Book of Ballet Stories* (1997), as well as contributions for BBC Radio 4, *The Daily Telegraph*, and *Ballet Review*.

Never Far from Dancing

Ballet artists in new roles

Barbara Newman

Routledge
Taylor & Francis Group

LONDON AND NEW YORK

First published 2014
by Routledge
2 Park Square, Milton Park, Abingdon, Oxon OX14 4RN

and by Routledge
711 Third Avenue, New York, NY 10017

Routledge is an imprint of the Taylor & Francis Group, an informa business

British Library Cataloguing in Publication Data
A catalogue record for this book is available from the British Library

Library of Congress Cataloguing in Publication Data
Never Far from Dancing: Ballet artists in new roles / Barbara Newman.
pages cm
Includes index.
Summary: "A collection of interviews with some of the foremost ballet
dancers of the twentieth century, reflecting on the paths that their
careers have taken since retiring"—Provided by publisher.
1. Ballet dancers—Interviews. I. Newman, Barbara, 1944–
GV1787.N38 2013
792.802′80922—dc23
[B]
2013021544

ISBN: 978-0-415-83214-4 (hbk)
ISBN: 978-0-415-83215-1 (pbk)

Typeset in Sabon
by Book Now Ltd, London

Printed and bound in the United States of America by Publishers Graphics,
LLC on sustainably sourced paper.

For Mickey and Beth – always near

The greatest music is never far from dancing.

George Balanchine

Contents

Illustrations

Acknowledgments

The artists who contributed to this book have created it, by speaking as honestly and eloquently as they once danced. When we first talked years ago, the social media that now shape so much communication had not been invented, and readers were not accustomed to dancers expressing themselves in words. Today, new technology allows performers to speak whenever they choose, but retired stars fade from public memory fast, and the insights they have acquired usually fade with them. First and foremost I thank these eleven dancers for sharing their thoughts with me so the dancers and viewers who follow us can share them too.

For their cheerful assistance with my research and patient attention to my detailed queries, I am also grateful to Rachel Branton, Natia Chachua, Clemmie Cowl, Rob Daniels, Torbjörn Eriksson, Miriam Eristavi, Eleanor Fitzpatrick, Francesca Franchi, Simon Harper, Majbrit Hjelmsbo, Marvin Hoshino, Angela Hughes, Gretchen Jax, Rebecca Lacey, Janine Limberg, Lady Lesley Mills, Laraine Penson, Nancy Reynolds, Stéphanie Rodier, Gabrielle St. John-McAlister, Thomas Beck Sørensen, Marianka Swain, and Sarah Woodcock.

Several photographers combed their files for images I was ultimately unable to use. So my gratitude extends as well to Nina Alovert, David Amzallag, Patrick Baldwin, Rosalie O'Connor, John Ross, Marty Sohl, Leslie Spatt, Martha Swope, and Linda and Jack Vartoogian for their time and trouble. Diana Davies and Jane Watkins kindly broke away from their own work to supply valuable editorial advice, and Vibeke Laursen provided a welcoming home for me in Copenhagen.

Only the tenacious efforts of Joan Brandt, Andrew Hewson and Stephen Morris enabled me to realize the original idea for this book, to which Ben Piggott and the staff at Routledge ultimately gave physical form and a public presence. As dance history moves ever farther from primary source material, I thank them all for their belief in the project and their commitment to it. Without their support, my attempt to document these dancers' lives would have come to nothing.

Note on text

The interviews appear in the chronological sequence of the dancers' births.
For the sake of clarity, reported speech is presented in double quotes and thoughts or unspoken comments in single quotes.

Introduction

Dancing lives in the present, arriving instantly and dissolving just as fast. Every step produces another, every gesture demands a response, nothing stops until the end. Dancers are the same. At every performance their artistry flows across the footlights continuously, minute by minute. Until the curtain falls they lead the public through a web of grace, power and illusion, strong as a bridge, enchanting as a dream.

Naturally, we never understand how they generate the effects that hold our attention. We can't locate the source of their musicality or dramatic conviction, and we never see their preparation, their fatigue or their fears, no matter how closely we watch. And one day, usually without fanfare, they're gone, and we lose the chance to watch them at all.

More than 30 years ago, when I realized that it was nearly impossible to discover what dancers thought about their work, I began interviewing them myself. I was convinced that no one knew more about their intentions than they did, so I asked them about the choices they made to satisfy their own ambition and, more precisely, the choices they made when they danced a particular role.

To my amazement, some of the greatest stars of twentieth-century ballet agreed to meet with me, not because of my reputation or track record, which didn't exist, but because the subject I proposed fascinated them as much as it fascinated me. "Good," said one of them with an approving nod, "you want to talk about *dancing*."

As the basis of my first book, *Striking a Balance*, that topic eventually introduced me to 27 artists whose careers spanned the century. The oldest had trained in imperial Russia and toured with Diaghilev; invited everywhere, the youngest could hardly draw breath between guest engagements and her obligations at home. The range of age and experience guaranteed that no two conversations would be remotely alike, but I hadn't anticipated that every one of them would allow time to stand still. As the dancers spoke, the past flowed into the present—Balanchine played the piano in the next room, Ashton lit another cigarette—and history became a private matter of commitment and effort.

Of course, time never stands still. Most of the older people I talked to then are dead; Felia Doubrovska died before the words she said to me appeared in print. Those who were still dancing were nearing the end of their career, and all but one of them have now given their last performance. And once dancers disappear from the stage, they seem to vanish completely.

Or almost completely. DVDs and old television clips preserve them as they were at their best, and you can catch glimpses of them on the Web, where their biographies tend to stop with their retirement.

But the dancers themselves don't stop. They simply move on, abandoning the spotlight and stepping into roles they might never have imagined.

Where do they go? What becomes of them? Immersed since childhood in the inescapable routine of class, rest, rehearsal, rest, performance, they have been guided, prodded, and supervised by others every day of their working life. Then suddenly, often unexpectedly, they find themselves confronting independence, and no one is watching. For the first time they are free to do whatever they want.

While time passed, many of the charismatic performers who'd once dominated the world's stages remained active but thoroughly invisible; others surfaced as occasional visiting artists or administrators. Yet the public never knew how they'd reached their new position or what alternatives they'd discarded along the way, and neither did I.

As attention shifted to younger stars and companies spruced up their repertory with novelties, relegating their heritage to scholars, I grew increasingly curious about the choices dancers make when time refuses to stand still. So after 30 years I decided to return to my original subjects and ask them about the intervening decades. I knew their comments would be representative, if not exactly random, and together they might illuminate a shadowy corner of dance that stage lights never penetrate.

Sadly, it was already too late to approach nearly half of them, who, since Doubrovska's death in 1981, had also fallen silent forever:

Lew Christensen in 1984; Toni Lander in 1985; Serge Lifar in 1986; Nora Kaye in 1987; Igor Youskevitch in 1994; Anatole Vilzak and Christopher Gable in 1998; Tanaquil Le Clercq in 2000; Niels Bjørn Larsen in 2003; Moira Shearer in 2006; Nadia Nerina in 2008; and Alexander Grant in 2011.

But eleven generous survivors again rewarded my curiosity with candor and trust. Although I wondered about the options they had considered, for the sake of continuity I figured the sensible tack would be to pick up our conversation where we'd left off so long ago, digging further into the topics and feelings we'd discussed then. But I quickly noticed that "then" didn't interest these artists nearly as much as "now," and that "now," as ever, meant the physical rigor and daily grind of honing practical skills for expressive purposes.

Perfectly comfortable in the studio and onstage, four of them were directing ballet companies, three of which are the flagship troupes of their respective countries.

Four more, universally renowned ballerinas whose individual artistry had exemplified their company's characteristic style, maintained equally individual links to their art, from full-time, hands-on involvement to almost none at all.

The remaining three—all British men, as it happens—were still connected to the dramatic roles they had created and the elegant standards they had embodied, though they too held enormously varied positions.

Decades ago I set out to understand the ways in which these performers were different, distinct as well as distinctive. To my surprise, their voices now identify some of the ways in which they are alike. With age they have acquired a new perspective, wider than their personal goals, and they focus their attention and energy on remarkably similar topics. The oldest and youngest artist insist on the same values in nearly identical words; an American woman and an Englishman, separated by style, repertory and an ocean, voice the same concerns with the same fervor.

Without disrespect, I have not mentioned their honors, titles, academic degrees or prizes, nor listed the books they have written, the books written about them, or their film and television credits, all of which can easily be located elsewhere. I've arranged their interviews chronologically to trace the sweep of history in which their careers developed. And I've tried, yet again, to pose the questions no one else could possibly answer: What hooked you? Who was important? Why take that path? How did you learn? A few protested, laughing, that they seldom thought about the past. But everyone spoke willingly, looking back to examine the choices that carried them forward.

Several of them have moved on again since they brought me up to date, so the present they describe here has already turned into something they couldn't predict. "The more I change," wrote Isamu Noguchi, "the more I'm me, the new me of that new time. To change is to invent, to create anew." These dancers didn't disappear at all; they merely reinvented themselves, out of sight but never far from dancing. Here's what happened next.

B.N.
London, May 2013

Alicia Alonso

Alicia Alonso (b. Havana, Cuba, 1920) took her first ballet class at 11 at the Sociedad Pro-Arte Musical in Havana. Arriving in New York four years later, she continued her training with Anatole Vilzak and at the School of American Ballet. She began her dancing career in the musicals *Great Lady* and *Stars in Your Eyes* and with Ballet Caravan. Having joined the corps of (American) Ballet Theatre in 1940, she was promoted to ballerina two years later. Although she maintained her affiliation with that company until 1960, she left periodically for guest engagements with the Havana Pro-Arte (1941–1943) and the Ballet Russe de Monte Carlo (1955–1957) and for regular appearances with the company she founded in 1948, Ballet Alicia Alonso, now the Ballet Nacional de Cuba. In 1943, following eye operations that confined her to bed for a year and a half, she made her debut as Giselle, a role with which she would be increasingly identified. As the first American guest artist to dance in Russia, she performed it with the Bolshoi and Kirov companies in 1958, later staging her own production for the Paris Opéra Ballet; she also performed the second act in Cuba on the fiftieth anniversary of her debut in the role. Though nearly blind today, she remains the director of the Ballet Nacional de Cuba, with which she danced her final performances in 1993.

§§§

Supported since 1959 by the government of Fidel Castro, who declared that "ballet, without any doubt, constitutes one of the highest and most beautiful of artistic manifestations," Alonso has always been a dedicated crusader on behalf of classical ballet in Cuba. She established the International Ballet Festival of

Havana in 1960 and the Alicia Alonso International Dance Competition in 1996, biennial events to broaden the performing context and personal contacts of Cuban dancers. Founded in 1962, the National School of Ballet in Havana grew from the fledgling academy she launched in 1948, and her own versions of the classics form the backbone of the Ballet Nacional de Cuba repertory. I spoke to her in Barcelona, where her company was performing her production of *Swan Lake* to packed houses. The Royal Ballet's Carlos Acosta, American Ballet Theatre's Xiomara Reyes, San Francisco Ballet's Lorena Feijoo and Joan Boada, English National Ballet's Arionel Vargas, and Australian Ballet's Yosvani Ramos were all trained, free of charge, at the National School of Ballet.

§§§

The most important thing was dancing. Dance. To do it better, to improve, improve, improve. I've been my worst critic. It was good, but it was bad at the same time. I never enjoyed it so much as other people—I could see they enjoyed it tremendously when they danced well. Every time I danced, some people would say beautiful things, but while they were saying those things to me, I kept thinking, 'But this didn't come out the way I wanted. This was not good. This should be better the next time.' They were very sincere, and I kept criticizing myself. That's my whole life as a dancer.

For me, to take a class was like a performance. I enjoyed every bit of it, and I worked harder and harder and I repeated everything with every group, one side, the other side. A class, that was my…breathing.

From my first Giselle to the Giselle after a long time, oh, what a difference! I kept enriching it and finding my own personality in it and my own taste and knowledge of it. I kept studying it all the time. I never stopped searching the books, critics of the time, anything that was written on that time of romanticism, for years I watched for them.

You know what helped me very much? Lithographies, and the way the dancers are standing, their poses. You can see what was the posture of their body and their head and their arms. This is important. The hardest thing for dancers to understand today is that you don't do everything the same way. The way you move your leg and your head in *Giselle* is not the same if you're doing a *Swan Lake*. It has the essential feeling of romanticism or of love, of sensuality. The technique is a medium, not the maximum, for an artist to express what you want to say, because you must dance with your technique but you must also speak to the people with it.

If we are talking about Ballet Nacional de Cuba, they have all the chances to develop, because I keep all the time reminding them of the different styles. There's a romantical style, a classical style, a demi-character style, and there's a ballet-modern style. They're different. And there's all kinds of different styles according to the great choreographers: there's a Balanchine style, a Fokine style, Michel Fokine, a Tudor style. We perform all year round, and all the dancers work very hard, otherwise I'd kill them! They need to be pushed...More than me? Well, nobody pushed me—I was pushing the poor teachers. I was asking them, Is this correct? Is this OK? But today...It's very difficult to speak in general, because this is a career that is so individual. But I can speak about our dancers in our company. They get a little bit spoiled. They're used to having maîtres de ballet, always rehearsing them and teaching them. They've got someone always in back of them, helping them and pushing them. I would get in a studio and I would work and work and work. Alone. By myself. I've told them that, and some of them do.

The thing I get trouble with is the classicals, because a classical ballet, like *Swan Lake* or *Giselle* or *Sleeping Beauty*, *Casse-Noisette*, any of those great ballets, is difficult to dance. You have to work, and to do something that is art, you have to work hard. Usually they say, "Why don't we do some modern ballet, something a little bit more free?" More free nothing! They just don't want to work so hard. Of course, I have danced modern ballets because I worked with Eugene Loring, with Agnes de Mille, with Jerome Robbins, my goodness...Balanchine...Carmelita Maracci...In one of her ballets, for the first time I had to smoke onstage, very bad, like a chimney. But I did just one little sip. I was doing the part of a spoiled, rich woman and went—one puff—and I couldn't stand it, so I gave it to another woman and she smoked for me.

The Ballet de Cuba has a very large repertoire. We have some modern ballets, but the Cuban audience, oh, they go crazy for the classicals. You don't have any idea how much they like it. You announce a performance of *Swan Lake* or *Giselle*, and it's full. Immediately the theatre gets packed. The *Swan Lake* you saw last night...of course, it's based on the original. But it comes too from logic, from the logic of a woman who likes theatre very much and understands the audience. I don't think the audience of today could stand all the four acts of *Swan Lake*. You don't need to do that pantomime, 'My mother's tears make the lake,' and the ballet would not lose the essence of the classical without it. The audience is able to follow the story very well, without the mother and the crying and the lake. You understand? That's what I do with the great classicals. I don't change them: I take the dust away.

We have combination programs, which are very good, and the dancers ask for them sometimes, because they feel it's different, they don't have to worry so much. They're interested in the classicals, but sometimes they worry that they have to work hard. Maybe they worry because I am very strict. I know I am. I respect very much the work. I respect the audience. You cannot...do anything and fool them and say, "Ha, ha, I got you, and now you clap." The most difficult thing for dancers is not to be looking for the clapping. Most of them are very happy when they hear clapping, which always is wonderful because it shows that the people are appreciating it. But you cannot get...we say "drunk" with it. No, no. I think you have to respect an audience tremendously, because you are giving them your art and your life and they respond to it. An artist gets into the mind of the people and he stays there, and he gives them many feelings, many ideas. Today, of course we need that. We need a breath of fresh air, very much, and art does that.

You know, the Ballet de Cuba is 60 years old this year. When I began it...I didn't look for something—I was looking for giving something. I know that a ballet company is very important for a country and for the people. It's an art that gives everything for them, and it's sort of like a dream that comes true, like they go into the theatre and see a ballet and they come out smiling. They become full of cleanliness and happiness, and you see them full of life, as if *they* were the dancers themself.

As you know, there was no company in Cuba. That was my dream always, and it did become real. In 1959, when the revolution came through, it gave us a theatre and a house for the company. They said, "What do you need for the company?" I said, This and that and the school, and from then on it's been growing and growing—today we have in Havana one of the biggest schools of ballet in the world. And we have a very large company. Right now we are dancing here and there's another part of our company giving performances in Cuba.

And we have smaller companies all over Cuba, and schools. Today you could talk about ballet in Cuba, and a taxi driver would say, "Who is dancing today?" I would say, So and so, and he would say, "Oh, that's a good performance. I will go today." A taxi driver! It's marvelous. That's the way it should be. Yes, Fidel has gone, but Raúl [Castro, his brother and successor] has come to the performances. We have the theatre, we have the company, we have the salary, we have the house, we have everything. Why should it change? Nobody's changed, not the people of Cuba and they are the owner. The people of Cuba are still there.

I learned to do this job by looking at what was happening with every company I've been in, Ballet Theatre, Ballet Russe…I kept watching everything. I was working together with my first husband [Fernando Alonso] and I knew that you could not become a dancer just by taking a few classes a week, not a real ballet dancer. They have to take it from when they're little and give their life for it. That was our dream and it came true when we made the school. In the very beginning there were some friends that admired us and they contributed to keep this going. We could not have the school the way it should be—we had *half* of the school. But after the revolution, everything came through. And that was it.

Now I like coaching and teaching and putting on the ballets. I have a very good memory, I learned every part of every ballet that I danced, the male dancing, the female dancing, corps de ballet. I wanted to know what everybody was doing so I knew where I was. So it means I could teach them, I could show them exactly every move. When Fokine worked with *Sylphides*, I would watch the way he worked, and *Carnaval*—he was divine. He was fat, with a little stomach here, and he would change into Columbine and into Harlequin. Antony Tudor was very good in that too, he could change his personality when he wanted. Now I can show a male dancer, a demi-caractère, Hilarion in *Giselle*, anything. But it's a matter of believing it, getting yourself into it.

And I also like choreographing very much, but this I learned from them and also from painters. They know how to put the equilibrium of a painting, it's fabulous, so that you can see where they want your eye to go. From painters I learned too the balance of the stage and space and color, and also the way to say stories, and I could grab that from Tudor too. And the way you move your corps de ballet I learned very much from Massine, Leonide Massine. I think I learned from everyone.

I made my first new ballets because...Before 1948 or before we did the company, I made little things for the school, to help the very advanced students. The company was made a little bit before '48 actually. Professional dancers came to dance with us, and then I made a little bit of choreography, but very little. But today I make it with pleasure. I *need* to do it. Since I don't dance myself I need to express myself through the choreography. And it's a wonderful feeling when I'm creating—it's sort of like I will be dancing. I do it in my mind, I work on it and I dance every single role. So I keep on dancing.

I've got many fantastic helpers. They know exactly my method, my way, my feeling. They've grown beside me since they are nine or ten years old, but I keep teaching them, helping them, and when I do choreography...I decide what I want to do, I seize the style for this ballet, and from all my helpers, my maîtres de ballet, I choose one that I know will understand it perfectly. They go to my house and we work for days and days with the music, with a camera, and writing. And me, I'm going, "This and this, and now they come to a lift and then they pose. Then she will do this when she goes to the back. Then at the end she walks and she looks, and the other one will take this..." I dance it myself practically, and they photograph, they film and they write down everything, with the music—I'm talking at the same time as the music goes. So when they go to the company, they start it right away, this and this and this. They don't have to wait for me to get again the inspiration. It's already done, and they have to learn it, quick—they don't lose time.

It is important for the dancers to have new repertory, because... How can I say? It's like you cannot always wear the same color. Let's dress in blue, blue, blue, there comes one moment you have to put on white, you have to put red, then green, because it stimulates you. It's the enrichment of words in your own vocabulary, your artistic vocabulary, and for the audience too, of course.

For me...When Balanchine did the choreography for *Theme and Variations*, for Igor Youskevitch and myself, I was very excited and very nervous. It was wonderful but terrible scary, because you thought, 'Oh my goodness, I have to do everything that Mr. Balanchine would ask me,' and he's very technical, no? He would say to me, "I would like you to do an entrechat six. You think you can do it?" I said, "If you want to, Mr. Balanchine, I do it." So I did it. OK. "Now do pas de chat, soutenu en tournant, double pirouette, demi-plié, pas de chat, soutenu en tournant, double pirouette. You think you can do it?" "I'll try, Mr. Balanchine, I'll try." "Good, good. Now, after that, you do…" Each time he kept putting more difficult and more difficult [steps], and then he would look at me and go like this [sniff], because he has a little nervous tic. I don't know what it meant, good or bad. I never found out. He never said anything. But he was incredible, a gentleman. To work with him was very soft and very quiet. But there was something very funny. Igor said to me, "He makes everything difficult to you, but my variation is so easy that any schoolboy can do it." And Balanchine heard it, and he came to the stage, "Igor, please come here," and he changed the variation. Then Igor said, "I'm sorry I spoke. It's killing me."

It's very important to help choreographers, because…It's very difficult to be a choreographer today, because no company allows anyone to waste time with their dancers because they have to pay for it. But we don't mind—we don't have to pay. That part of expense is already taken care of, and we can afford it. But we think too that it's important to create new things, because we have to give for the future what was our life today, like the great classicals did for us. We have to leave *our* way of life, our way of thinking and feeling, a rich history.

Actually, dancing, and arts in general, are like a big tree that makes fruit, and this fruit is for everyone. How can you give them fruit? By taking it to them. You cannot stay in one place—it would be selfish indeed. We just finished a tour in Egypt, we danced in front of the pyramids. And the Festival in Cuba is wonderful, because I give everyone a chance to meet each other. When we're on tour, we're just running around, around, around, and we don't meet everyone that we would like to meet. At the Festival the dancers talk, one to another one, for a long time, and critics are together there, it's a very good feeling.

In the Ballet de Cuba they enjoy dancing…and that's not everywhere. That's the trouble with dancers. Sometimes they forget they are not dancing for themselves, they are dancing for an audience. We make our dancers very conscious of this: you are dancing to give your art, not to receive. You're giving to the people. The way that we work them on the style makes them different too. For instance, we even teach the corps de ballet, when they're going to walk and do a pose, they must wait…take a deep breath…and then pose. We teach them that: insert a moment. This is just a small detail. And we teach them the style of the head and the arm. *Swan Lake*, the arms back and the head sidewards. *Giselle* is forward, over, like this, round arms, yes, and body forward, and a pure classical, *Sleeping Beauty*, is noble, straight. And *Don Quichotte* is absolutely completely different. They must, they must, start with the style, not mechanical but with art. And also, the feet go with the timing, with the beat, but our arms and our head go with the melody, not stiff but continuous.

There are many important things. They mustn't forget that when a man and a woman are dancing together, he is the man and she is the woman. He's helping her, but he's not just there to hold her—they are dancing there *together*. And another thing is that in the corps de ballet, each of them is a personality. In *Giselle*, What are you? Well, one of the friends is in love with one of the other friends. And you are the son of a certain person, and you work in the graves. [And you,] what do you do? Oh, I like to make wooden things. OK, you look at the wood and it's different for you. We make each of them have their own life, so they project their own life when they're projecting this ballet.

Also, we make them understand the story and be part of the story, not let only the principals do the story. They have to do it too. We are very strict about the way they do every role, the way they walk, the way they behave. It's part of their training and it's part of their personality. Who is their model? Me. And the teachers for the school are from the company. My goodness, 60 years of training, 60 years of company and more years of training before that, we have made many good teachers. We have teachers all over the world practically.

The school has 20 rooms to work in and treatment and everything for the students. And they get complete schooling, so when they finish the dancing or if they want to change career or if they don't improve enough so they really wouldn't make a good dancer, they can go to the university because they're prepared for it, so as a human being they haven't lost time. They study for eight years and then they do one year or two years of pre-training, professional, to see if they stay in the company or they go to another company. That's the way we do it.

In the school, they do a little bit of folklore [dance] and they learn music, they learn French, I think, and they do a little bit of theatre. Not jazz or modern, no, because I think what they learn as a ballet dancer prepares their body to do any kind of dancing. When a choreographer comes with a style, any style, you have to know what he wants and then communicate with him and start doing his choreography. The dancers will learn it. Their body is ready for it. It's a matter of the dancer himself wanting to do it.

You know, I don't like competitions. I don't completely agree with them, because they make the very young dancers do things sometimes that they are not up to. I've seen many people get hurt because they're not ready; they feel like they're ready and that's not true. But I know that we need these competitions to stimulate the teachers and to stimulate people to learn to dance—that's the way to awake many places about ballet dancing. So the competition… it's necessary for the public, not for the dancers, and you have to do it. There are certain things that sometimes you don't agree with much but you have to do. It won't kill anyone, so OK.

Television too. Of course it's good that the audience will watch it, because sometimes the people don't understand the steps and they think, 'What are they doing?' Yet they get used to looking at it and then they begin to understand it. They learn it by watching, and then they get curious to see the whole thing in the theatre.

What will happen to ballet in the next 30 years? You know what? It's the same thing that will happen to all the good art. It will still grow, because it's one of the most wonderful things that men can do, really beautiful. Art is something that goes into you, into your mind but physically, and it gives you ideas to do other things that are more practical. It's a stimulation in your life, it gives you life inside. It's important. And ballet is the mother of all the dancers. Well, when you take ballet and you do the exercises of ballet, you can do any kind of dancing, because you dominate your whole body. I know—I've done it myself. I've done Spanish dance, I've done modern dance, I've done folklore dance, I've done ballet dance, I've done every kind of dancing. But of course I dominate my body, I can do anything I want to.

When I used to dance, I was floating like…I was creating every part of it, I was transported. When I do choreography, I begin to get the same feeling. I go to another world, so I keep on dancing. When I go to see a performance, I dance it with my muscles. They contract with the music, because I know physically, Here come the fouettés, Put your back straight. And I *push* but I enjoy it…but not so much, because I wish I was there, pushing more.

I think I have a strong character, I *must* have it, because I've been very stubborn about making a career. But I try, when I teach my dancers a role, not to impose my way of dancing, my way of feeling it. I impose on them my own knowledge of how you can do it one way or another way or this other way, always in the style, but I let them choose their own way, so they will project their personality. When you see a prima ballerina or a premier danseur, they will do the choreography, but they don't lose their personality. I'm very careful about it, because I'm very conscious about that. I think the beauty of a company is to see how many different ways you can project in one ballet. Like you can see many *Swan Lakes* and in each of them, a ballerina will project a little different, will *give* something a little different.

I give them my experience, my whole experience as a dancer, and as a human being too, because it goes very much with the career. You have to think your life is your career, and if you love your career you have to really live for it. And it's worth it, it's worth it, because everyone has to have a line to follow in their life, and that way you know where you're going. You have your way, your route, already made, your line is there. If you get out of it, you may get lost, and then you waste time in your life. You know your line because it's the one you like, the one that attracts you. When you look at it—I'm talking as a dancer—you think, 'What will hurt my career? Well, it will hurt it if I don't sleep enough,'—I'm talking physically now—'if I smoke, if I stay all night outside and I go out to parties, if I don't take classes, if I don't work, if I don't keep on rehearsing new parts, new things.' That's physically, that's every day.

'And I must go to museums, I must see what all the artists do. I must learn from paintings, I must listen to music, not popular music but great composers and what they did with their music. All that enriches my life.' That doesn't mean that I could *only* do that— that means that it was the most important part of my life. Maybe I would take a moment away, just having laughs in the house with some people. But my life was…I think for a dancer…and I think for anyone, really, the important thing is to find what they love to be in their life and do it and dedicate themselves to it. And don't waste time, really enjoy it. It sounds like, Oh my goodness, what a terrible life. No! Because I enjoy every bit of it.

Barcelona
May 2008

Beryl Grey

Beryl Grey (b. London, England, 1927) entered the Sadler's Wells Ballet School at the age of ten and joined the Sadler's Wells Ballet at fourteen. Awarded leading roles almost immediately in *Les Sylphides*, *Façade* and *Les Patineurs*, she danced her first complete *Swan Lake* on her fifteenth birthday and made her London debut in *Giselle* on her seventeenth birthday. She then appeared as the Lilac Fairy in *Sleeping Beauty* in the company's opening performance at Covent Garden in 1946 and, for the first time, as Aurora and Myrtha later that year. Mastering a repertory that extended beyond the nineteenth-century classics to de Valois' dramatic *Checkmate* and Massine's humorous *Le Tricorne*, in her first ten years with the company she danced 43 leading roles in 32 ballets. In 1957 she resigned from the newly christened Royal Ballet to freelance around the world; later that year she became the first British ballerina to appear as a guest artist with the Bolshoi and Kirov ballets. After retiring from the stage in 1977, she served as artistic director of Festival Ballet (now English National Ballet) from 1968 to 1979.

§§§

Having already put her dancing and directing careers behind her when we first met in 1979, Grey became, during the following 30 years, ever more widely involved with dance. Along with staging the classics and occasional teaching, she has given her time and experience—as a director, chairman, vice-chairman, president or governor—to such organizations as the Royal Ballet, Birmingham Royal Ballet, the Royal Opera House, the Royal Academy of Dance, the Imperial Society of Dancing, the Imperial Society of Teachers of Dancing, the Dance Teachers'

Benevolent Fund, the Dancers' Resettlement Trust, and the Royal Ballet Benevolent Fund. To accommodate her hectic schedule, we rearranged this second interview several times, and when we finally sat down to talk in a quiet corner of the Royal Opera House, she could only spare an hour between other appointments elsewhere in the theatre.

§§§

I hadn't planned anything, actually, after dancing. I didn't think of it. I always left everything to fate. I don't know about dancers today, but all I was interested in was the next performance and what new roles I would have. I was very happily married, and I'd always said I'd stop when I was 40. And then I was invited by Grace Cone and Olive Ripman to take over the Arts Educational schools, out of the blue. It took me a year to decide whether to do it or not, and then I thought, 'Well, that would be nice,' because it would keep me in the world of dance, because their children were used by what was London Festival Ballet for their *Casse-Noisette* and for other ballets if necessary. I've always been interested in the education of dancers, simply because, I suppose, when I was in the Sadler's Wells school in '39, Ninette [de Valois] started to give us very interesting weekly classes in the history of dance. And when we came into Covent Garden in '46, we were extremely excited, because you felt you were stepping into the shoes of all these great ballerinas and the aura of their wonderful performances, which I'd seen here as a child student. So I felt the history of dance was terribly important, and because the Arts Ed. had a teacher training college...You know, the accent today is very much on what the public's seen, which is the dancer, the modern dancer, the experimental dancer. But the important background to all this is the teacher, and what you get onstage is the product of dancers being trained. I felt that by taking on the Arts Ed.—I was still dancing—I would be dealing with the education of the dancer and I would be still in touch with the profession.

I was always very conscious of how lucky I had been in *my* teachers, because I had Madeline Sharp at my little prep school. I suppose she was about 20 or 21, and a pupil of Phyllis Bedells, and Phyllis, of course, had studied with all the great Russians. So my teacher, from when I was six, used to send me to Phyllis; I had two sessions of six lessons, so I had 12 lessons a year from Phyllis. And then when I went into Sadler's Wells [school] when I was ten, I had

[Nicholas] Sergeyev from St. Petersburg and Ursula Moreton and Ninette, both of whom had been with Diaghilev.

So I took over those schools and I enjoyed trying to relate education and art. [The students] would paint and, on the drama side, they would act. The other thing that had always impressed me, even as a child, was the musicality of the Russian dancer, and I felt that the dancers in Tring needed desperately to have some musical background, so they were all given recorders. It was a wonderful start, and after two years we had a little orchestra.

Anyway, since I stopped dancing…Well, for six years my husband was so ill I've had to turn down so much recently. But I love staging the classics. There's greatness in them. Wonderful pure choreography and an affiliation with the music; because the music was written for them, they are perfectly aligned to the music. But also the stories are very dramatic and very inspiring. And you've got the tradition that they have been danced by the greatest dancers that we know about. Dancers *love* to do the classics, because it's the greatest test because they *are* the most difficult to do. They demand a keen, pure technique—you can't fudge—and you are continuing a tradition, so in the leading roles you have a great responsibility. And each dancer will bring their own interpretation. I first did the whole of *Lac* when I was 15, Act II when I was 14, and when I stopped at 40, my very last performance was in *Swan Lake*, and there were *still* areas of it… You were constantly discovering and exploring ways of giving your own interpretation through movement. It's a challenge technically, emotionally and dramatically, and I suppose that's why they live on. They are the top of ballet, the crème de la crème. The music lives on, the story is as relevant today as it was then, and they're beautiful. They add a little beauty to a rather ugly world.

Four years ago English National restored [Mary] Skeaping's *Giselle*, which she'd handed on to me to produce. I worked with Agnes Oaks and Tom Edur, the most wonderful artists, what a loss to the company they're going to be. And like me, they wanted to have a meaning to every movement. You see, when you start, first of all you are challenged by the technique and you learn to build up your strength. Then as you grow into the role, and the technique should then become of a lesser magnitude of challenge, what I found is that your time is taken up with interpretation. So you're not just doing steps for the spectacular result and pleasure of the audience. You are doing that *plus* giving each movement a meaning, a reason.

I don't think you learn other than the steps from the video, and dance should be more than just steps. That's what I feel—she says, unkindly—about choreologists. Choreologists are invaluable, and they can safeguard the choreography. If you look at a film, you again see the steps, not always clearly, not as clearly as a choreologist can give them. But it's the contents, it's the soul of the dance that is important, and that's what a producer should find and try to develop in each dancer, his or her own particular strengths and weaknesses.

I think we've advanced technically enormously over the last 20 years. Legs are very high thanks to Sylvie Guillem's inspiration, and pirouettes go on forever, particularly when ballerinas are partnered. The partners, the men, are much better at pushing them around. And there has been another important development. In the '50s you had a clear demarcation line between contemporary, like Martha Graham, and classical ballet. Well, thanks to Nureyev, really, and Baryshnikov...They were the first two great artists to bridge that divide and bring the two together, and I think ballet has benefited enormously from this, because it's freed it up. I'm coming back now to the importance of teaching. Some teachers can produce very good technicians, but the freedom of body involvement and inspiration is very often tightened and restricted by the technical demands of ballet. The modern has given a better understanding of the dancer's relationship to the ground, to space and emotion, and an ability for the body to move in many directions, not just in a straightforward way.

You have to remember that classical dance was developed at a time when...Well, the dancers wore corsets up until about the '20s, so the leg height was extremely low, and that's why you see these lovely, flowing lines of Karsavina and Pavlova. I think one of the dangers today is that with all these great technical advances and the lightweight, diaphanous robes and the leotards that dancers wear now—in other words, unrestricted costume—they have to be careful not to lose, in the joy of movement, the actual reason of being onstage and doing a series of movements.

I think costume is dreadfully important...Take a hunting scene, for instance: they'll move around but they won't necessarily hold their bodies in the right way. Now, you put them in a period costume, and they *are* restricted. You put a woman in a skirt, and she's at once more feminine and moves more gracefully. The difficulty in something like *Giselle*...In the Romantic period, the woman was very much dependent on the man. Now the balance has been brought up; the men are important, and the woman is just as important and has very strong movements. If you go back a hundred years, the women weren't allowed mental freedom, and their whole attitude was to be reliant on the man. So the whole angle of the body and the head *has* to be slightly more forward than today. If someone isn't totally confident, you'll notice they don't stand upright. Today, all the dancers are upright because they're very confident, they've been well trained, well looked after...They may be very nervous, but they have a confidence. So the neck and the head movements become terribly important and the arms absolutely crucial but *not* stretching out. I find teaching *Giselle* so difficult, because dancers want to stretch and elongate, but the Romantic period was very withheld. The woman was very shy, very conscious of her femininity, she has to be much more within herself and the movement's much more delicate. We aren't living in a delicate age now, and it's very difficult for the dancers to get that angle. But once you get it, it's very exciting.

I must say, when I was helping revive it for English National Ballet, it was wonderful to see the change in each rehearsal—I'm thinking of corps de ballet at the moment. The principals tune in and understand much more quickly, but for the young dancer who's doing everything energetically, to be told to restrain, to restrict the movement, it's a completely different attitude. But dancers always want to learn, at least I hope they do. I think we all want to learn. We go on through life learning. If we don't want to learn, we might just as well be dead. I had a marvelous teacher in Audrey de Vos. Quite a few of us from Covent Garden went to her. She was quite ahead of her time, and she was able to pass on to each dancer the interest in the relationship between a movement and what part of the body was involved and what that movement would actually be for. That was very interesting.

You know, I was married to a doctor and he always used to say how stupid we were and how blind. I remember the first time he saw me backstage; you're pouring with perspiration when you come off, and nobody would think of putting a shawl or anything 'round your shoulders. He said, "You're all building up trouble for yourselves. Can't you look after yourselves?" But now dancers are much more aware of what they're doing to their bodies.

When I came in in the war, that's when I suppose ballet started getting spread to people who wouldn't normally have gone to it.

Before the war it was really for a minority public who believed that only the Russians could dance because of their temperament and so forth. When the war came, audiences for entertainment grew because people wanted a form of escapism, whether it was the Anglo-Polish [Ballet] or Rambert [Ballet] or going to hear Myra Hess in the National Gallery giving her lunchtime concerts. We all danced right through the war and we were very conscious of the increase in numbers and the interest shown by even members of the Forces, and that was quite extraordinary.

I was president of all the dance societies, there were about 12 of them across the country in the war. These were small groups of people who were sent lecturers, and when it was possible Ninette would let some of the dancers go to perform. They would have maybe a pas de trois and a pas de deux sent, that was the only way of getting to learn about dance. So after the war, there was… not a large public, but a much bigger public who had developed an interest in dance. Now it's so available, and the audience are much, much more educated, aren't they? Heavens, the chances they have of seeing dance…There's television, you can tune in on Sky and see performances in New York, in Italy, in France—gosh, the opportunities—or go to films even. And on ads, dancing is used all the time. Dance has become part of life in a way it wasn't 40 years ago. Most companies, modern and classical, offer talks before performances, so they introduce to the audience the background of whatever they're going to see. The audiences have grown, I think, to an extent that they are really raising the standard, because they are seeing so much and they can begin to discern what they like. They may not know why they like something and why not, but they can discern the difference between good and just ordinary.

People mustn't be snobby about dance. I think *Strictly Come Dancing* is wonderful, of course it is, what's wrong with it? It has brought dance into homes in a way that very few other things have done, on an enormous scale. It's done an enormous amount for dance, in the way that Wayne Sleep did. He had that wonderful program on television [*The Hot Shoe Show*] many years ago, bridging the musical comedy and the ballet, and that did a great deal of good. You see, people must be allowed to *enjoy* dance. That's one of the problems with ballet: people still think it's elitist, and it isn't at all. There's no such thing as elite in dance. Dance is basic to every human being.

What has been so interesting, over the last 20 years, is the development of ethnic dance in this country. The Imperial Society [of

Teachers of Dancing]—I'm the Life President—they now have a
section for Indian dancing. And there seems to be a great resur-
gence of interest in Greek [dancing]. It's invaluable for youngsters
who want to begin to learn to dance. People are not afraid to step
outside borders like they were. You know, everything used to be so
constricted...restricted...constrained, and if you did Greek maybe
you shouldn't do tap, and if you did tap...Ninette was totally
against my doing tap, she believed it weakened your ankles, but
of course it is invaluable for people to feel rhythm and begin to
understand and enjoy rhythm.

That's what's wonderful about...You come into Covent Garden
on Saturday mornings and you see these groups of little children
being shown all around the theatre, and they can take classes...
There's so much done in the schools too. When I was running
Festival Ballet I was the first person—I'm told, I didn't realize it
at the time—to send out a little group to schools to educate them
a couple of weeks before we would come, say, to Southampton or
Liverpool. We had six dancers, and they would talk to the children,
show them the shoes the men wear, the shoes the girls wear, the
tutus, give them a tiny little history and show them a few steps at
the barre and a few steps in the center, and finish up doing Bluebird
or a variation. That has really taken off. I mean, you get money
from the Arts Council if you have your educational group, and I
think that's exactly what the Arts Council should be doing, funding
the education of young people.

It seems to me that dance, art generally, always takes a back
seat in politics. It's difficult for politicians, because you've got the
elderly to look after, you've got the young to look after, you've
got health problems, immigration problems, education problems,
you've got to run the country and cope with problems internationally, so I quite understand why dance does come down rather low
on the list. People think those things are rather more important, and
I understand totally. But dancers should be leading the politicians,
controlling the politicians, but we're not. Now the politicians are
controlling the artists. I don't think they have time to listen, really.
Each successive art minister comes in with the best intentions, but
we don't seem to get anywhere. There's no Lord Goodman [former
chairman of the Arts Council of Great Britain] anymore and Jennie
Lee [former arts minister], that was the time when we had support.
You have to have a politician that totally believes in the importance
of art, and until the politicians understand and realize that...Maybe

it isn't even them. Perhaps it's their constituency, who think that art is frivolous still. I don't know, but we certainly need to speak with a much louder voice and push much harder. Well, the will is there but not the time. I know when I ran Festival Ballet I never had a second. But with all the education that's going on in colleges and these degrees that are given out, surely these people could speak for us. There aren't that number of places for dance managers and critics, everything's being cut back and cut down. You'd think they could do that.

I'm very happy to talk about dance now, I'm very happy to give the odd masterclass, but I wouldn't like to teach every day. It's very draining, and you have to bring something fresh. It's a calling, and there aren't that many wonderful teachers. It's a very demanding and responsible job, particularly if you're training a talent for a professional career. It's an enormous challenge. I taught quite a lot in the past, and I go abroad and give classes, and I enjoy that. One wants to help and pass on what one's learnt, and I want people to enjoy movement and dance and music—music's very important to me. I'm not really a musician; I just play the piano. I've just moved and at least I've got my grand piano in. I wouldn't have taken the bungalow if it hadn't gone in.

Yes, I've judged some competitions as well, and I think they have the same value as examinations, really. Dancers have to get used to appearing in public, they have to get used to controlling their nerves and to competition. Because life *is* competition, and if you're going into *any* area of the theatre, or if you're a poet or a painter, there's nothing wrong in being ambitious. If you want to be better, then that's marvelous. It makes you work harder, it raises the standard of your performance. I'm all for competition.

The one thing that I would say against competitions is that...I go back many years now. It's very easy for a teacher to train a dancer or a couple in certain solos or pas de deux and bring them up to a certain level. And I do think it's important that the dancers are given other work to do which isn't pre-set, so that the judges can see how they respond and the speed of pick-up and the artists' powers of creativity. I was president of the All-England Sunshine Competition for years, ever since the war, until we lost our secretary and it was shut down. We had the children right up to about the age of 20, and I used to give a class, so you could judge that dancer very quickly, and then you saw what they did when they'd been trained in a certain solo. I don't do them now. And I'm no longer a governor of [this] opera house, because of my age. I'm over 80. They won't keep you after 75, I'm afraid.

Oh, I don't think anyone needs me. There are thousands of people, I'm sure, who can do good. I still chair the Royal Ballet Benevolent Fund, and we do help a lot of ex-dancers and performing artists when they have accidents and need operations. Ninette started the Benevolent Fund in '36 with Arnold Haskell, and it was for ex-dancers of her company, the Vic-Wells Ballet, as it was called then. Now we've extended our activities so that we help all dancers that come within the criteria for hardship. Not just ballet [dancers], they're in all the dance companies, all the contemporary ones. The smaller the company, the more help they normally need, because they can't afford a dancer to be away very long and they can't afford health insurance for the dancers. Then there are lots of older dancers, who are either ill or financially in problems. So we help quite a lot.

The Dancers' Trust [now the Dancers' Career Development], I'm on that, is basically for retraining. The commercial dancers in shows like *Phantom of the Opera* need a lot of help. They're out of work for many years, you know, it's a very dicey career. It's all luck of the draw, fate...I come back to fate again. But [this organization] are wonderful with dancers who will be wavering, they don't know whether they should stop their career. Maybe they've had illness, maybe they've not got a job, maybe they've had an accident, and this woman, Linda Yates, tries to interest them in areas where they might have a talent.

When I was running Festival Ballet, one of my ballerinas took up flower arranging, and quite a few become osteopaths. I had one or two men in my company that wanted to become masseurs, and they hadn't got their...what was it called in those days? A-levels? They actually had to go and do the A-levels before they did the study to become masseurs. It was amazing, but they were willing to give up something like four years. That's one thing we help with: we don't pay for training, but if there's, for instance, a man who is married and has children who has had to give up his career, the Dancers' Trust will perhaps give the money for the actual training fees. But then, what about subsistence? What about the mortgage, the wife, the children? So that's where we come in again...if there's hardship.

When I had a baby in 1954, I only had a month's pay and then no pay until I returned. Everything's changed very much, thank goodness, in every country. I don't know if it's always for the better, but...I mean, dancers have better rehearsal rooms because perhaps there's more money about or perhaps management's realized it's in their interest to provide better conditions. At English National and this [Royal Ballet] company, they have a masseur and all that sort of thing. We didn't have anything like that...no, that's not true. After the war we did have a masseur, but we were still rehearsing in church halls when I left in '57. So things have advanced very rapidly. The public have come to expect better conditions, and the artists therefore expect better conditions, and their unions have demanded them.

I don't know if they've improved, necessarily, the standard of dancing, but they've improved their quality of life and their expectancy of life when they've finished dancing; in other words, they won't be crippled and they won't be financially derelict, as it were. There are pension schemes...When I took over Festival Ballet in '68, my dear administrator [Wilfred Stiff] was absolutely horrified there were no pensions for dancers, and he was the one who got it off the ground. We were still doing what Ninette was doing when I joined the company in the war, and that was paying the dancers every Friday, in cash. And then, it would have been about 1970, this administrator said, "This is ridiculous. They must all be paid by check. It's absolute nonsense."

I think ballet has made enormous strides. The care of dancers, training people in good eating habits and the dancers' awareness of their bodies has happened. Mark you, I still think dancers smoke like chimneys. And the conditions...the unions have stipulated the actual degree of warmth that the studio must have; the dancers don't have to perform in a studio or on the stage if it's not at a certain temperature. Those things are important if the dancer is going to live on and then return what they have learnt, as a teacher. So many of my friends left saying, "It's such a relief not to do barre and get up early every morning and have sore hips and aching muscles and bleeding toes." Then after a few years, they miss it all, and a lot of them want to take up teaching. The RAD [Royal Academy of Dance] have this very good teaching course for professionals...That's another thing: the standard of teaching *is* improving because more dancers, who wish to go back and teach, are actually trained in the fundamentals of teaching. You're either basically a born teacher or not, but there are certain fundamentals which are valuable if you're going to teach and have your own school eventually. With one or two, experience is all that's important, but I'm thinking of maybe your corps de ballet girl or boy—a certain training adds confidence. I always needed the confidence of going to my private teacher [de Vos] and having coaching, so if you're going to step into a new area of dance, it gives you confidence to have a little basic information fed to you. And you've got to give confidence to your pupils, so I think it's very important, I'm all for education. You learn all the time. Even if you don't like your teachers, you then think, 'Why don't I?' so you've learned something.

Oh, ballet matters so much. It's a form of escapism, it takes people away from the crudity and ugliness of life today, and one hopes, if it's a great performance, that it renews their spirit and soul, gives them strength to go forward. That's what I've always believed. *I* think it will go on. I hope it will. I'm sure it will.

One of the great developments, and the reason I don't think ballet will die, is the way that it is proving itself to be able to engage people of today in situations of today. It isn't just able to be dance in a tutu. If you look at some of the modern ballets, they're fantastic. Have you seen that new one of [Wayne] McGregor's [*Infra*]? And we've become interested in lighting ballets, we've been much more aware of modern design and architecture, and ballet is beginning to involve itself in these different mediums. The use of these mediums is important but it is exciting too, and I think that's why ballet will live on. It'll adapt to the age. I mean, art reflects its age, doesn't it? Whether it means to or not, it has to, inevitably. We won't go on creating tutu ballets in the sense of *Swan Lake* or *Sleeping Beauty*...though Fred did a marvelous classic; look at *Fille Mal Gardée*. One or two of his ballets, I think, will live on, like Balanchine's and *Dances at a Gathering*, pure dance, and some of the Forsythe ballets, pure dance, wonderfully musical. It's the relationship between movement and music which I think will guarantee the future of ballet. That's my feeling, anyway. I'm probably quite wrong.

And it's nice to see so many young people. At concerts, don't you notice the difference? I do. I love going to concerts, and it does impress me there are a lot of young people. It used to be very stuffy. I used to listen to the Hallé [Orchestra] in the war up in Manchester, and there were very few young people, it was predominantly the older generation, and I can remember thinking, 'Oh, this is all old people.' Of course a lot of youngsters were fighting then, I know.

Goodness knows what will happen to me. I just like to be asked advice and be in touch and see performances. I enjoy watching the ballet. My great love is opera, of course. I adore opera, absolutely adore it. Oh, I need that. If you read some of Ivor Guest's books about the Romantic period, it's interesting how many of those great Romantic ballerinas became singers when they were 25, 26. I would love to have been a singer. In my next life I definitely must be a soprano. I would love to sing *Traviata*.

London
May 2009

Donald MacLeary

Donald MacLeary (b. Glasgow, Scotland, 1937) began his ballet training with Sheila Ross in Inverness shortly before he entered the Sadler's Wells Ballet School in 1951. In 1954, he joined the Sadler's Wells Theatre Ballet, where he created leading roles in Kenneth MacMillan's first commissioned work, *Danses Concertantes* (1955), and made debuts in both *Swan Lake* and *Giselle*. Having launched an enduring partnership with Svetlana Beriosova, he became a principal in 1959 and transferred to the Royal Ballet at Covent Garden. Within his first ten months there, he danced *Sleeping Beauty*, *Sylvia* and *Coppélia* and originated major roles in MacMillan's *Le Baiser de la Fée* and Cranko's *Antigone*. Best known for his repertory of noblemen and his sensitive partnering, he also performed with distinction in such diverse ballets as *Song of the Earth*, *Apollo* and *La Fille Mal Gardée*. Having announced his retirement in 1975, he remained with the Royal Ballet as ballet master until 1979 and then appeared with the Scottish Ballet and several other companies as a guest artist.

§§§

Donald MacLeary devoted nearly his entire professional life to the Royal Ballet, so when he says "the company" that's what he means, and when he says "here" he means the Royal Opera House, where we sat and talked outside one of the rehearsal studios. Between our first conversation 30 years ago and our second, he returned to the company in 1981 as a *répétiteur* and became *répétiteur* to the principal dancers four years later. He retired from that post in 2002 but continued as a guest in the same position until 2007.

§§§

It's a very weird thing: I never really thought ahead. I only thought about what I was doing at the time. Obviously I was getting on when we talked before. I was 38 and I had an Achilles tendon operation, and I thought, 'Well, that's it.' And Kenneth [MacMillan] said to me—he was the director then—"Would you consider being ballet master?" and I said, "Yes." I didn't realize how successful that operation was going to be. Otherwise I might have said, "I still want to go on." He said, "You can go on dancing if you want to," and I said, "I don't think I should do that, because it's a big job and I'm new to it." He'd asked me to rehearse David Ashmole in *Romeo* and I helped Desmond Kelly in *Swan Lake*, so I'd been in the rehearsal room and I was quite enjoying it, and I think they were clocking on that I was quite good at it. And at 38, I'd been there for something like 25 years, and it's sort of like leaving your family. You're so caught up in them all, and they're your friends too. I couldn't have left. The theatre's too much in my blood.

I have to say, giving up is a bit like coming off drugs. I've never been on drugs, but I couldn't *not* wake up, brush my teeth and stand in second position. So I said, "No dancing," but thank god I kept going to class every day. Anthony [Dowell] went off, so I had to get up and do *Swan Lake* with Makarova. And in New York I was rehearsing *Song of the Earth*, and David Wall went off on the day of the show, and I had to go on with Makarova. I was fine—mind you, the next day my body was in total spasm, but I had to do it again that night, I did them all. But that's because I went to class.

Actually, dancing's a great leveler. If you're an actor, you walk in, do your show, you have the rest of the day off. The dancers do the show, and then they're in class the next day at 10:30—I mean, that's a discipline. It's one of the hardest professions to be in, because you have to have the right framework, you have to have musicality, you have to have passion…You don't have to have all those things if you're an opera singer. You can be fat—it doesn't matter. Joan Sutherland once said to Margot [Fonteyn], "You've no idea what it's like singing with a bad tenor. It's ghastly, just terrible." Margot said, "Imagine dancing with a bad partner. At least you can go on singing. If he drops me, I'm on the floor." You have put your trust in that man, not like singing. It's dangerous, some of the stuff we do.

The Americans would understand the job of *répétiteur* more as a coach, but that sounds a bit athletic. But it's important to me that dancing's not athleticism only, that it is theatre, it's an art form—it's not going for gold, it's going for the hearts. I'm interested in getting people to become artists and not just dancers, and I liked teaching them how to partner properly. I'm a bit upset when I see paddling. I mean, a good partner...you shouldn't know what he's doing behind the girl. Why do you have to push her through 24 pirouettes? And the music waits—aaaaaahhhhhh, boom! It's awful, and that's what worries me about some of the performances I see.

As a dancer, I always wanted to tell a story as best I could, because no matter how well you dance and how well you partner, if you don't tell the story they're going to get bored. I used to concentrate on that a lot. One of the first influences on me was Robert Helpmann, who was Margot's partner and also a Shakespearean actor and a contemporary actor, he did everything. When I went with the touring company to Australia in '58–'59, I did Laertes to his Hamlet and I was rehearsing for *Swan Lake* with Lynn Seymour. And he coached us, and because he was very theatrical the emphasis was on the theatre and telling the story. He taught me to be still and to use my eyes and not be moving all the time.

That made you think about things—you know, Why am I doing this? Listen before you look—simple things, but a lot of people don't think about them. When I'm rehearsing people, I say, "What did you come on for? Why are you going over there? I want to see *how* you go over there and why." I was also very impressed with Albert Finney in *Tom Jones*. It made me realize that even if you have a period costume on, you're still a human being. People were doing princes like cardboard characters, nose in the air, and not looking relaxed in the clothes they were wearing. But I thought, 'I'm a real person, although I've got this costume on.' I find all that important, and a lot of it gets lost.

You prepare yourself to coach by learning, first of all, from the people who are doing it to you. And I learned how *not* to do things by being coached by certain people. You have to encourage—you don't tell people how ghastly they are. When I was being coached by Michael [Somes], I thought, 'If I ever do it, I would never be so horrible and cruel.' He had discipline, but he was verbally cruel to people. You need the discipline, but you have to do it with encouragement. I'll give you an example of Michael. He'd been asked to come back [to the Royal Ballet] to put on *Symphonic* [*Variations*], and I was put down [on the call sheet] to be with him and I wondered why. So we did the rehearsal and I said, "OK, see you tomorrow," and he said, "No, it's up to you now. I'm going up to Birmingham. I'll see you on Saturday." So I worked two casts, he came on Saturday morning and the first cast did it, and he leaned over to me and whispered, "Very good, dear, but I'm not going to tell them." Then he got up and slated them. "Very good, dear," because I'd got it, and then he crucified them. What's the point?

So you get experience through your own career, but when I started to coach I just went in and did it. I didn't really have a person that I thought of as an example. Ninette [de Valois] was pretty amazing to be rehearsed by, and Fred [Ashton], and Kenneth, and Helpmann, they all sort of influenced me. And that was very important because it was the Royal Ballet—it wasn't an international ballet company. When I was young, it was mainly Brits and colonials; we were all very much trained the same way, and it was "The Royal Ballet," with very theatrical people in it and theatrical narrative ballets. We all were taught to act almost straightaway, all Ninette's ballets were story ballets, you grew up doing things like that.

Now it's a bit different. A lot of people come in from other countries, and they're very good dancers but they're not Royal Ballet dancers. Some of them can become it, and others don't want to. They come because the rep is so good, and then some decide, 'Well, I'm not doing it *that* way.' I've had somebody say to me...She'd been thrown on in *Romeo*, and Anthony and Monica [Mason] had helped her. Months later the same dancer was scheduled to do a performance of her own, and I was to take her for the rehearsals. She said, "I can't remember a thing about this," because she'd only had the one, and I said, "Don't worry, because I know it backwards." By this time, you know, who hadn't I done it with and who hadn't I rehearsed? Within five minutes, I said, "No, that's wrong," and she said, "Well, I didn't do that last time." And for an hour and a half she challenged me and challenged me and challenged me. I said, "I know you were pushed on, we're all very grateful. But I was an original Romeo and I worked with Kenneth and I've looked after the ballet for him, I know it." And she said, "But things change." So I don't rehearse her anymore. She won't have me. And she did exactly what she wanted to do in the performance. A lot of people wouldn't know and they would think 'Marvelous. She's a marvelous dancer.' But it's like coming along to do a Mozart concerto and changing the notes.

It's easier for me if they're in the company. If we have a guest artist in, there's no time. I won't say to them, "You're not doing that properly" or "That's not right," because they're in and out. But, say with *Romeo*, [Roberto] Bolle was here for about three weeks before his show, and I said, "I'm going to help you," because he was doing...They all do it like a Kirov dancer, posing away instead of being Romeo, or like they're doing *Sylphides*, standing still. But it's not a classical ballet—it's a twentieth-century ballet, and Kenneth wanted you to be like a real person. Bolle listened and he was very good, and [Igor] Zelensky the same. I kept saying to him, "Look, you're not doing *Bayadère*. You're meant to be a passionate young man." They all think 'I'm the lead, look at me,' and everything's the same. That's why I'm worried about the company losing its identity. I was very passionate about keeping whatever made the Royal Ballet what the Royal Ballet is.

I'll tell you who I thought was amazing and Kenneth thought was amazing, for awhile, was Sylvie [Guillem]. But she hasn't left a role that ballerinas are going to be wanting to do, like Lynn Seymour has. I think Kenneth would have done [a ballet for her], but he went right off her, because...Well, she sacked me as a coach very quickly. When she first came over, I coached her in the classics, like one does, and she was amazing and intelligent. But Kenneth went over to put *Manon* on in Paris, and he didn't choose her for the first performance. So she's done it [later] in Paris and she's now coming to do it with us, and I'm rehearsing her. And I think, 'But that's wrong.' "This is what we did in Paris." Then I go, "Well, that's wrong too." "This is what I did in Paris." Part of it was so fast, I turned to the pianist, Philip Gammon, and said, "Have you ever played it this fast?" and he went, "Never." "This is how we did it in Paris." So I felt like a coat hanger in a rehearsal room, and I thought, 'I'm shut out, but what do I do?'

Another thing that she did, she changed a lift at the end of the balcony pas de deux in *Romeo*. They're not all doing it properly because it's hard to do, but you shouldn't lift the girl straight up—it should go first to the side and around, sort of curved. Well, they changed it to the lift in the *Manon* bedroom pas de deux—it looks like 'Take me, I'm yours.' Kenneth said, "What are you doing? Why are you changing...?" and she said, "But I'm doing one of your lifts." And he said, "But don't you realize, Juliet's a virgin and Manon's a whore."

People's personalities are different. Some people are like a sponge. You get some that can't wait to be told what to do and how to do it. The insecure ones, funnily enough, are the easier to teach. It's the confident ones that are more difficult, because you have to work very hard to get their trust, and then they'll do what you want, but you have to *prove* it. Thank god I could still do things. A lot of the boys say, "I can't do that. My arms are too long," and I'd get up and show them, you know, lift the girl or pirouette the girl, and embarrass them into thinking, 'Well, if he can do, I ought to be able to do it myself.'

I put on two new Romeos this season—I always do both the men and the women—and one of the Romeos was a foreigner. He did a pirouette with his arm here [in front] and I said, "No, the pirouette's with your arm up," and he went, "I can't do that." I said, "But that's what rehearsals are for. You work on it to get it right." Then there was a lot of I can't do this and I can't do that, and I finally said to him, "When I was a child and you'd say, 'I can't do that,' the teacher would say, 'There's no such thing as can't.'" So he did it in the end, but it was a *sweat*, because he wanted to do it another way or cut out things. They all try and cut out things, because they're hard. Especially Act I of *Romeo* kills them, and they cheat. I won't let them cheat.

It helps that I've been through it myself because I can say, "I did it. If I can do it, you can do it." I had a boy in *Les Sylphides*, and in the solo there's an arabesque pirouette with one arm up and then an en dedans pirouette with both arms up, and it's to the left. And he said, "Why can't I do it to the right?" I said, "Because it's choreographed to the left." He said, "I'm a right turner." I said, "I was a right turner too, but from age 17 when I first did *Les Sylphides*, I did the turn as it was."

Everybody's a different person, but they're all waiting for you to tell them how to do it, oh god, yes, you've got to come up with the answers. If something goes wrong, I am the one who has to get it right. And now I don't think they practice on their own. When I was about to do my first *Swan Lake*, I used to get on the stage and practice like mad because I used to get very nervous, and the more you do, the less nervous you get. There is the odd one or two who are a bit lazy, mainly boys really—they haven't got the patience the girls have, I don't know why. Males are probably on the whole a little bit lazier than women. That's why women make better directors than men. I'm not saying that Fred wasn't a good director or Kenneth wasn't a good director, but they didn't enjoy it. Whereas Ninette enjoyed it, Monica enjoys it, Karen Kain [at the National Ballet of Canada]…she loves it, so she's good at it.

I don't go down memory lane with the dancers, because they don't want to know how hard it was in the past. But when I first joined the company there was no physiotherapist, none. You went off and paid for treatment by yourself; Elsie Wareing was the great one that everybody went to. Now we have god knows how many people, and I feel—this is a personal thing—that it's like a vicious circle. It's a huge responsibility for the physio to say, "OK, you should go on tomorrow," because they might not have got it right. So they always err on the cautious, "Take a week off." I mean, I had cortisone injections in the morning and danced in the evening. If they have a cortisone injection now, they have a week's rest. But again, they don't want to hear about that.

They would say that what they have to do is much harder now, but I don't think it is. We just did it, and we didn't give in to it so quickly. We didn't dare, because Margot was standing there, at the end of *Symphonic* for example, as if nothing had ever happened. You know, it killed Rudolf [Nureyev], doing *Symphonic*. And I've taught *Romeo* to Baryshnikov and [Irek] Mukhamedov and Zelensky, and they're all on the floor at the end of that balcony pas de deux, they don't know what's hit them. I've had Derek Deane in a rehearsal learning Romeo, and he used to stop at the end of his solo, before that pas de deux, and say, "I can't go on." So I'm getting frantic, because I always say, "If they fail, I fail." And I'd go, "Today, you are not going to stop. Go on, go on, go on!" and at the end of it, he went and threw up behind the piano. Then he went to Kenneth and asked him to get rid of me; he said I made him so ill he had to go to the doctor. And then he becomes this great disciplinarian, apparently, as a director—everybody said how tough he was.

The training we had...it worked for a lot of us. We all managed to get the work done. The other thing too is that you can train people to a good standard but they're not all going to make it, because there isn't a Margot Fonteyn every year or a Rudolf or a Carlos [Acosta]. They don't grow on trees. Monica once said to me, "You must be so thrilled with Darcey [Bussell]," and I said, "Yes, but I'm more thrilled that I get people like Belinda Hatley up to do Aurora." Because Darcey's got a Rolls-Royce engine, and Belinda doesn't. So it's like getting a little jalopy up to Rolls-Royce standard, and I get more out of that because I've had to really work. When Belinda, insecure, gets up and does beautiful work... and there've been a couple of others. They're usually the ones that really listen, but they don't have confidence, and I feel that it's an achievement to have given somebody the confidence. And it's only by encouraging. Michael Somes used to say, "Do it again. Do it again." His theory was that the more you did it...Well, if you're not doing it correctly...So I always say, "I'll go away and think about it," and I'd come back the next day with a different way.

You're very critical when you're a dancer, you get so pickety. It's very hard for me...This morning the third-year girls and the third-year boys [at the Royal Ballet School], the seniors, were doing classical solos, and they do the steps but they don't dance. They don't use their heads or their bodies. They turn and they jump, and they don't put their head down or up and they don't bend. When they're doing a waltz, they go like this [arms out to the side], and... no head. No dancing. Not what I call dancing—it's not just technique, you have to dance. That was what was so wonderful about Fred—he expected you to *move*. And he hated to see a preparation, and now they go...

One boy doing Colas [in *La Fille Mal Gardée*]...The preparation was from fourth [position]. He pointed to second and pliéd in second instead of jumping into fourth. And I said, "But it's from fourth," and he said, "But I've been trained to do it in second." I said, "But you've been trained to learn choreography. If you do it in second, you're late, because it's taken you two counts to get there and plié. Whereas you should plié, pirouette, *attitude*, *attitude*, with the music." It took me *forever* to get him to do that. But you see, the other really important thing is the musicality. It sounds awful if the orchestra are suddenly waiting or taking big rallentandos because the dancers are doing something that they shouldn't be doing. It *kills* me. All of them want it at half-speed, because it's easier.

I'm only working with the principals, I'm only rehearsing a pair, so I'm very conscious that the pair has to get it musically right, because otherwise it doesn't work for me and it doesn't work for you and it doesn't work for anybody. But I think it all depends who you've got as a conductor, too, because your life is in their hands, actually; as a dancer, they are controlling you. Sir Malcolm Sargent did a new orchestration of *Les Sylphides*—this is a long time ago—and...it wasn't good. But he came to rehearsal, the pianist was playing my variation and he was doing this [conducting with one hand], and then he said, "Fine, see you tomorrow night." Well, the principal boys dressing room was one floor above the stage, one floor up. When the boys in the principal dressing room heard the speed of my mazurka, they all were able to come down before I'd even got on the stage, it was so slow. It's heavy anyway, but my legs when I came off...I don't know how I got through it.

And you couldn't just go ahead. It's always better if they go too fast, you can cut things out, but it was so slow. Then I realized that the [rehearsal] pianist knew the right tempo, and Sir Malcolm just didn't take it in.

But slow is the fashion now. We've inherited that from all the Russians. Some of the Russian conductors are terribly sweet, and they go, "But I was waiting for her," because they've been trained to follow the dancer. There were conductors that you could trust. John Lanchbery was amazing, and Ashley Lawrence was amazing. But there was another one, Emanuel Young, and I would think, 'Oh my god.' I used to say to him, "Just set the tempo. Don't follow me," because I would go slow because he was going slow. I remember doing endless performances of *Raymonda*, all across America, and saying to him, "I don't want to do it that slow."

I must tell you about those tours. I did my first *Swan Lake* with Lynn in Australia...Philip Chatfield and Rowena Jackson used to do Monday night and Wednesday night. Then we had people fly in for a while, and when they'd all gone, I'd do Tuesday night with Lynn and Wednesday matinée with Susan Alexander, for the whole of the rest of the tour. That's what I don't tell people about going down memory lane, but what I do tell them...There's always something you get out of a different partner, and the more you do it, the more you think about how you can do it better. That's what I try and get across, because some of them...Wayne Eagling's the worst: "I don't want to rehearse. I've done *Swan Lake*." So I used to partner the girl in rehearsal so she'd have somebody to work with, while he went off and played golf. But you have to want it. I've always wanted to be good and wanted to be better and not settle for a platform. You have to always be thinking, 'What else is there in this that I can get out of it?'

I didn't have to learn any of those ballets—I knew them from watching. But nowadays, they don't watch other people dance, I don't think they watch at all, so you have to teach them from scratch. That's why they don't always get up to the top, because they're not hungry enough or passionate enough. But actually, the advantage that we had over them is that we toured a lot, and they were long tours. They wouldn't want to do them. We were six months in Australia and two months in New Zealand, and we used to do long American tours. Well, the longest they do now is five or six weeks, so the disadvantage is that they're not getting the chance to do the role often. And the same here [at home], they share, so they're only doing one performance out of five, and that is hard for them.

When I was with the touring company, we did a 22-week provincial tour, and that's eight shows a week, traveling on Sunday. We used to book our own digs...Somebody gave us a list, we wrote off for the digs, carried our own luggage from the train...Kenneth, Cranko and Peter Wright were choreographing; it was Peter Wright's *Blue Rose*; Cranko did an abstract ballet [*The Angels*], it wasn't very good, we never did it very much; and Kenneth was doing *The Burrow*. I was in all three of the ballets, and we used to rehearse in church halls with pillars and things. Well, they just wouldn't do it now. The new studios here are fantastic, all of them, but they go, "I hate this studio. Why aren't I in another one?" But that was all we had, so you had to do it...and you wanted it.

The repertory now...What we're not getting is good narrative short ballets—young choreographers don't seem to be able to do that. And the other thing I would say about choreographers is they choreograph for themselves. Kenneth choreographed for the person he was working with, you felt you were really involved. But Ashley Page, Wayne McGregor, all of them, they're dancing it themselves. They don't say, "Show me." *They* do it, and you have to copy, so you're not creating a role. Same with Chris Wheeldon—he shows Darcey what to do. He's written it on himself, and when you see him doing a solo, *he's* doing the solo—it doesn't come out of her. But I thought Wayne McGregor's one [*Chroma*] was amazing. I said to my partner, "Do you realize there are four Auroras up there?" I think they were *incredible* to do it, because you couldn't get a modern dancer to go out and do Aurora. The hugeness of the capacity of what they're doing is amazing.

Things that are written for them—fine. But things that they come into, as I said...Things change. That will happen. Bits will drop off or bits will get added or somebody will do something and they'll vow it was always there. Because who's in control? Any new work that comes along now is automatically written [down]. The rep I coach...Well, eventually...We don't all live forever. Having done these ballets is the best tool for coaching, really. I lived with them for so long; the music always reminds me and my memory, which is hopeless for other things. I only seem to concentrate when I'm in a rehearsal room, and I get very tired because the concentration is huge, you can't stop. When you're a dancer, you're doing your bit, then she does her bit so you're having a rest. The person that's taking the rehearsal is doing both bits and everybody else's bit as well. So your hour and a half rehearsal is concentrated, then you get somebody else in for another hour and a half, and you're on the whole time. It's very tiring.

I don't like them looking at too much video, because...a lot of times...The videos are done at rehearsals, somebody starts to mark so they're not getting the right thing, somebody changes something—"Oh, [Alessandra] Ferri did that." I say, "I know Ferri did that, but she changed it." And they sometimes see things that I wouldn't encourage them to do: "Well, so-and-so did it on the video," and I say, "But it's not good." If I know the ballet, they don't have to go to the video. Those two boys that I taught *Romeo* from scratch, I taught the whole thing, and the Juliets as well.

Another example about videos and speeds is that I was judging the Adeline Genée Gold Medal for the Royal Academy of Dancing, with Antoinette [Sibley] and [Irina] Baronova. It's the so-called "British school," and they were all doing the Royal Academy syllabus. They did a bit of class, then they came to do their solos, and it was all broken wrists, arabesque up here, very high, and their arms up by their ears, and very slow. I said, "They've all been watching Russian videos." I think it's the teachers—I might be wrong, but the teachers watch [videos] together. I said, "It's really because their teachers are all these Russian dancers, and they're doing Russian solos," and Baronova said to me, "Oh, don't say Russian—it's Soviet." You see, there is a big difference. We learned from the Russians when Sergeyev came over, and then [later] they were in a timewarp and getting slower and slower and cutting out mime.

When I first saw the Russians, when they came over [in 1956] with Ulanova and did [Leonid Lavrovsky's] *Romeo*, Kenneth and I went together, stood at the back, we all thought it was absolutely wonderful. Then gradually I kind of lost respect for them, because they're just machines and they go from one beautiful position to the next. You never see anybody bend sideways. They can bend back, they can get their legs up, they can pirouette, but they don't move me, and very often the partners don't communicate with each other when they're dancing. That annoys me so much, because they've got all the facility but they don't think of why they're doing it. It's the same old thing. It's not, 'Why do I do that step?' They just think, 'How do I look?'

Here I never stop going on about Why did you do that? or What made you walk over there? and That's not the right step and This is what Fred would like. I am telling them what *I'm* expecting and hoping that they'll give it to me. You have to get it out, that's what rehearsals are for. They can come in and not move at all, and then I say, "You're not dancing. I haven't seen you use your head, I haven't seen you use your body." I find the same in class, in the schooling. I think the teachers iron out the natural dance quality that some people have, and they all become a bit of a machine. They all come in stiff, and they walk like this, like Coppélia. If you tell them to waltz, they can't waltz. I mean, it's called *dancing*. I know you have to get a technique, but you can't do the whole thing without moving.

And the other thing, if you've got a bad teacher...There was a man I saw in Canada teaching the last-year students, and his arms were appalling. Well, you learn by copying; you see somebody with dreadful arms, you get dreadful arms. That also worries me. I've had to do other things at the Royal Academy, and one of them was judging girls that had been on the Teachers Training Course at the Royal Ballet School, judging them as dancers. These would-be teachers had to dance, and some of them could do fouettés and some of them could hop for hours on one pointe and some had sickle feet. Other teachers came in to watch from all over the place, and those teachers said, "Why did you mark *her* so low?" I said, "Because an opera singer has to dance with his voice, and a dancer has to sing with his body, and she wasn't doing it." One woman said, "But her floor patterns were very good," and I thought, 'Well, how sad.' All they have to do to be a teacher is to pass an exam—you wouldn't have passed any of them, really—and then they're responsible for teaching people of the next generation, and they've never been in the theatre and they've never danced in a company.

It's stupid, passing exams. I mean, girls who groom horses have to pass an exam. What for? You might be brilliant at passing the exam and your stable management is hopeless, whereas someone else can't read the paper but she's brilliant with the horse. Thank god we didn't have to go through these assessment classes, when I was at the school we didn't have anything like that. But we were younger when we went into the company—I was 17—and you kept learning as you went on. And we were so lucky that we had teachers that been in the company or, like Miss [Winifred] Edwards, had danced with Anna Pavlova, and Fred, who'd been influenced by Anna Pavlova...we had *theatre* people. They don't have them at the school now. Miss Edwards used to say to you, "This is the classroom, and that's the front." She talked about "Face the front"—not face the mirror, face the front. "Take the audience with you when you do a grand jeté." She related the whole thing to the stage. Now I never hear that, I *never* hear that. I hear, "And a one and a two and a three and a four, and a one and a two and a three and a four…" And when they're doing a grand jeté, they *don't* take the audience with them.

The dancers say, "I've got to get my leg up, because it's expected of me." We were talking about *Giselle*, and I said, "I want to see you make me cry. I don't care what height your leg is." I think *that's* what the audience want, to be moved. You can get people that aren't such good technicians that can move you or somebody that's not moving you, and you think, 'Yes, she can get her leg up, but so what? We've seen that before.' So it's going back to artistry. You have to forget about technique and get on top of artistry—that makes the audience interested, so they want to come. There's nothing like the live theatre. It's like these crazy football people going to Moscow to see [a match]—why not watch it on television? It cost them a fortune to get there, but it's a spur of seeing the real live thing and being there. So you should always have a goal of being as good if not better than you were the last time. You shouldn't be thinking about applause or how many curtain calls you get or anything like that. That's not part of being an artist.

London
May 2008

Lynn Seymour

Lynn Seymour (b. Wainwright, Alberta, Canada, 1939) studied ballet in Vancouver before winning the scholarship that
brought her, in 1954, to the Sadler's Wells Ballet School. After
joining the Royal Ballet Touring Company in 1957, she created
leading roles in Kenneth MacMillan's *The Burrow*, *Le Baiser
de la Fée*, and *The Invitation*, and in Frederick Ashton's *The
Two Pigeons*. As a principal of the parent company at Covent
Garden, she continued to originate major roles, for MacMillan
in *Romeo and Juliet*, *Anastasia*, and *Mayerling*, and for Ashton
in *A Month in the Country* and *Five Brahms Waltzes in the
Manner of Isadora Duncan*. She left the company several times,
initially to dance with the Deutsche Oper Ballet, Berlin, under
MacMillan's direction (1966–1969), then to direct the Bavarian
State Opera Ballet in Munich (1978–1979), and often to perform as a guest artist internationally. Although she retired from
the Royal Ballet in 1981, she returned to the stage seven years
later to appear with English National Ballet, Northern Ballet
Theatre, Second Stride, on tour with Nureyev, and in Matthew
Bourne's *Swan Lake* and *Cinderella*.

§§§

A steady source of inspiration for Kenneth MacMillan, Seymour
began to explore choreography herself when she collaborated
with Robert North to create *Gladly, Sadly, Badly, Madly* for
London Contemporary Dance Theatre in 1975. Having made
several pieces for Sadler's Wells Royal Ballet and the Rambert
Dance Company, she choreographed her last work, *Bastet*, in
1988. She began teaching in 1981 and has taught since then as
a guest of the Paris Opéra Ballet, Sadler's Wells Royal Ballet,

Rambert Dance Company, and in Zurich and Houston. She has also coached the classics and her own roles in Britain, France, America, Italy, Germany, and Canada. She was briefly the director of the Greek National Opera Ballet (2006–2007), and spent two years studying at the London School of Psychotherapy.

§§§

It was *The Red Shoes* that hooked me. It's banal, isn't it. I had two things happen to me at once. I saw that film and I heard, sitting in the middle of a beautiful forest, all the Beethoven symphonies on a kind of marvelous reproduction-of-records machine. And I just thought, 'In order to live, I have to be in this world, with these elements around me.' I was about 12 or 13.

The most important influences on my dancing? There are three. One of them is Frederick Ashton, one of them is Rudolf Nureyev, and the other one is Stanley Williams. All men. And to some extent, Margot Fonteyn. Sir Fred was a wonderful ballet master, and I worked with him a great deal, very fortunately, on ballets that weren't his, *Swan Lake* and *Sleeping Beauty* and *Giselle*. He danced images in front of your eyes…no, he spoke images that danced in front of your eyes. He used to put Spessivtzeva there, same with Pavlova. He said, "She was like a wild woman," in *Giselle* Act II, "we were terrified of her." I tried to do what he told me, and I got so much from that. And also from working with him as a choreographer, because he always first of all did the ground plan of what the variation was going to be. "You travel from that corner to this corner, now in this phrase you stay in place, now we'll make a circle, now stay in place here," that sort of thing, and then we'd make the steps. He told me that first; well, that *is* the choreography actually. How far you go in a certain passage denotes everything in the little in-between steps. If you have to travel a long way, it immediately gives you a dynamic that would be different if you only traveled half the stage. It was the secret of understanding Petipa to a very large degree, and it also made you know where you were on the stage and where you did something vital. You couldn't just do it any old where—it had to be in a very precise spot. This was the most amazing dancing lesson, because you're not taught that.

Rudolf took it upon himself to show me what classicism was, because I didn't know. He showed the world, actually, not just me. Well, me and the world, but I was a willing slave to his ballet mastering. I didn't have to be singled out, I was quite happy to be included. He thought that if you cheated you weren't being true to the classic—that's why he was so exacting. I thought, 'I've got to learn this because I like breaking the rules,' but you need to know what the rules are first so that you can do it more efficiently. I like playing around with those premises but I didn't realize what the basics were. And I didn't realize how vitally important they also were to the technique, what the turnout was really for. Turning out gave you stability and made you able to move quickly and to do things that you can't do when you're not spiraling in this way. It all fitted in together with the person he then led me to, which was Stanley Williams, the great genius teacher.

These were quite simple things these people gave me. They seem awfully obvious, but...Rudolf was there to teach me about the purity and the fundamental beauty of the classical technique, the simplicity, and how it should be honored. This is why he and Margot got on so well. He could see it in her; her simple way was *so* direct and she was such an honest worker. Here I have to talk about Margot, because her influence was in the class, not on the stage, because she would gather all the elements... She was given an enchaînement and before she practiced this exercise she would, in her head, fix up the head, the arms, the eyes...how it would be presented onstage. So when she came to do the exercise, she was trying already to make it a stage-worthy presentation. Everything was encompassed—she wasn't just going to work her legs. That takes a lot of...concentration, to make it how it should be as a finished product, to make the whole thing work as one, all the time, and she was marvelous at doing that. I used to just look and look and try and emulate and emulate. And also, she was always there. She did not ever miss class. When she was older she used to leave a little early, but she would always try and stay for a grand allegro unless she was absolutely whacked or aching.

Rudolf's example...There was nobody else. They didn't know like he did, and also, they didn't want to know in a way. Lots of people didn't like Rudolf, they were offended by him. Well, he was forceful and critical. He was offered the directorship of the Royal Ballet *if* he stopped dancing, and he said, "I need to keep going." It was an idiotic thing to ask him. They were thinking—I guess they were trying to be democratic in art, which is always a mistake—that some of the other boys might be upset. Well, tough! That the people that do the hiring and firing think like this is just astonishing. They have an extraordinary record of not backing the right horse for all sorts of weird reasons. Anyway, he went to Paris and look what the Royal Ballet missed out and look what he did for Paris.

The other thing about Rudolf is his generous heart, which can't be overlooked in our profession. He was one of the only people who not only criticized me very harshly but also loved my work and talked to me about it and would tell me the good and the bad. And I respected his opinion so very much that all other things paled, actually, in comparison. If he thought it was lousy he wouldn't mince his words, but if he thought it was really worthy he would also say so. They were my happiest times in my career, working in the studio with Rudolf. We just clicked there, because we weren't in any kind of competition, we were just working away with rather difficult bodies and we were both late starters. We had very similar problems, really, the catch-up game, always having to make sure it might work.

Rudolf led me to Stanley. I'd actually heard about him before from Peter Schaufuss, who I worked with briefly with ENB [English National Ballet] and the Canadian ballet; Stanley, of course, was his teacher. So it started...By this time I was in my thirties. I phoned up the School [of American Ballet] and begged them to let me come to his class, which I did, twice a day, whenever I was there [in New York], and sometimes I went there specially. They were very kind to me at the School, really sweet, and so was Stanley. My first class was a boys class in the morning, but he put me behind a girl...The company used to come and take his class, you see. Violette [Verdy] was there, Merrill [Ashley], everybody was there. So I was put behind this girl who was a veteran of his teaching so I could...get the message slowly by the way she was showing and doing. And then, I was a goner, because it was truth all boiled down to the "B of the Bang," the zero. It was just beautiful, a sort of intellectual and physical nirvana in terms of body movement, and you went into an area of concentration that was fantastic. I learned to dance then. I finally was getting a technique. I didn't know before. I was just struggling. So it was an absolute revelation, a joy actually.

A mathematician or a scientist might understand it, because they're into refining theoretical...Now, we're working with a body. Presume the ideal body's equal on each side, and you have to work the two sides, and the turning out is about the two sides working equally. It's not a position, it's an action all the time, and that's what makes you turn. To use a force one way you need to use another force the other in order to maintain your equilibrium. And the moment of departure…it's like mathematics: if you make a mistake there, at the absolute beginning of a phrase, then chaos will ensue eventually. If you don't get the *départe* right, the turn might just about work, but it will be hard for you, so you'll use more energy than you need to, which you really can't afford to do.

I was involved in the [Royal Ballet's] Choreographic Workshop, not as a choreographer but as a guinea pig. I offered myself readily because I love doing it. After I'd [performed] two or three for a couple of friends, I thought, 'This is great. I'm going to try one myself.' So I did a thing called *Two's Night Ride* and I got a commissioned score and I had live music…After this one, Kenneth [MacMillan] said, "Now try a bigger one," because I'd just used two people. So I thought, 'OK. I'll do more.' It's the same as creating a ballet when you're a dancer—I liked both roles. You're part of that creative process, and that creative time was the thing I enjoyed above all else. I preferred that to performing actually, because by then it was all over. I think what I got from choreography I already knew, I don't think I learned anything more… except some fairly disappointing things. Because you're dealing with lighting designers, costume designers, technical staff, directors, it's hard to realize the image that all creators have in their heads, people always want to cut corners, they never give you enough time, they say "This is impossible, it's the money…" So all the lessons I learned were very nasty ones and not very useful for when you're a dancer, except you appreciate a little bit that this all has to go on.

I stopped choreographing because I got pissed off. I had some things interfered with in a way that depressed me, and I thought, 'How can these people do this, to me or to any creator? How dare they?' They were, in a way, quite silly things. In one piece I'd created, *Wolfi* [for Rambert Dance Company], the middle movement was all choreographed around these big flowing capes. Then they wanted me to rehearse a revival after it was first on…They'd removed the cloaks. I said, "Where are the cloaks?" The director, who's a choreographer himself, this was [Richard] Alston, told me, "The dancers were having a little bit of trouble with them," and I was treated like a real troublemaker for getting a little bit upset about it. I was absolutely speechless.

I had [always] done quite a lot of outside stuff. In the '60s, for example, I did *Seven Deadly Sins* in Marseilles. I did a lot of guesting in Canada, I did a new ballet evening with Félix Blaska in Paris, I worked with Roland Petit in Canada, I was in Berlin…I danced all over. I kept leaving the Royal Ballet. The reason I was restless when I went to Munich was that there wasn't going to be any new work. That's *why* I went to Munich. Evidently the intendant wanted a specific person [as director] who dropped out, so I was second best. They turned out to be extremely unhelpful, but it was again an interesting process, and I was able to promote a lot of new choreography during the time that I was there. Billy Forsythe did two pieces for us, including the piece that put him on the map, *Love Songs*, and I was promoting young choreographers all along the way.

It was a bit of thick and thin, learning that job, especially as I was left in the cold. The intendant wasn't helping, and it was a giant house that had all its own people who fight for position. I had a little experience from Berlin, and I knew it wasn't a straightforward process. If you had a lot of people on your side you could work wonders, but making any changes in working methods in these places is like changing the constitution, you're working against a lot of odds. I wasn't very successful in doing that. It was a bit stupid really [to accept the job], but I thought it would be very interesting. And don't forget, I had three children, all of whom I put through school. I wasn't married, I was by then nearly 40 years old, I was having to find a way to make my career longer. My youngest child was only just starting school. One forgets that one's earning…it's *not* completely for oneself. From that time onwards, actually from 1968 when the twins were born, I was doing a lot of work, not for me. And of course, when you're doing that you're also trying to do something that makes it palatable for you—otherwise, how really dreary. But the guiding force behind many, many decisions was providing for my boys.

You need some kind of consensus as a director. But I also think that the dancers in many companies have been abused and they've made a lot of strict rules in order to protect themselves. They're abused because they're treated, not like fellow artists and creators but as sort of minions, and I think this is a hangover from the days of the *petits rats* and the tsar's scullery maid's dancing daughter. The administrators want a success, and most of them don't know what ballet is. They know what opera is, so they see success in

ballet through the eyes of opera, they think ballet runs the same
as the opera does. You come in as a director, you're the enemy of
both of them, dancers and administrators, if you want to make
any kind of changes, because they've got their rules that make it
tick over. In these opera houses in Germany, they do seven performances a week, the theatre's never closed. It's a kind of machine
that gets cranked up and along it goes until August. It's very easy to
exploit the dancers in these situations. So because of being abused,
they've managed over time—I'm not saying yesterday but over the
century, up to when I went there at the end of the '70s, let's say
it's 70 years—there's been a little democratization. They've got a
union, they work specific hours, they won't go on the stage if it's
below x degrees of temperature, they won't go outside to another
rehearsal room, they have to have this much time for lunch. And
the administration want a genius to come in and work under those
conditions and become an overnight sensation.

I think the circumstances haven't changed in many houses.
They're still the same as in Munich, so you go into the same kind
of situation. In Greece it seemed like it might be different, because
the intendant was new and wanted…My brief was that they wanted
to create a new company for a new opera house, but in fact, again
they wanted me just to go in and make a big splash, with the exist-
ing rules and regulations. They only work 20 hours a week, and I
don't mean each person. I mean you only have 20 hours a week in
which to work! So I was there for three months and I handed in my
notice, because I knew they weren't going to budge. I was engaged
for three years, but I thought, 'This is pointless. I'll become an old
lady far too fast.'

When I [first] retired [from the Royal Ballet], I was still in good
condition dance-wise, I could still choreograph and I had experience in directing. I hadn't taught up to that point, but I thought
probably I could. But I was disenchanted and I remarried, for the
third and last time, thinking that I might actually have a normal life
ahead of me…well, I got married two years later. I hadn't met the
man at that time, so he wasn't part of the decision-making. I didn't
want to be with the company anymore because…I wouldn't be able
to stand it actually. The teaching was dreadful, there was not going
to be any kind of repertoire except me at 40 doing Juliet, which I
thought was absurd…

Then I went back, because my marriage had failed and I still
had three sons to put through school and I needed to go to work.

What else could I do? But I really hated dancing then. It was hard, I didn't want to be there, I felt that I'd done it all, and...it was torture. I don't think my approach changed much. I was probably more firm in how I went about things. It's something that happens when you get older because you don't care that much, that's how you do it actually, "If you don't like it, you can get somebody else." I mean, you're professional and also terribly responsible—that never goes. You're not going to turn out a bad show. But it's probably a more intellectual effort than an emotional one. The physical [effort] is enormous because the maintenance process is extremely hard, from 50 onwards, and that makes dancing very hard indeed.

Teaching doesn't feel like an adjustment, because you're just telling the people what you tell yourself and trying to make clear what the big hurdles are and what the basic absolute necessities are. How you go about doing it is actually up to you. For instance, I have never taught children. The youngest that I've taught are old teenagers. So you have to deal with where they are in their training, because lots of people haven't had very good early training. So you're starting with a sort of semi-adult, trying to get them to catch up, but I know a lot about that and it was probably quite useful. The first place I taught was Danceworks, one of these studios in town. They were professionals but they weren't all ballet dancers. Some called themselves professionals...you got quite a cross-section of rather interesting people. I got very fond of them. There were all sorts in there, and they were very attentive and brave and good fun too.

Then Rudolf asked me to come and help him in Paris. He was putting on his *Romeo*, which I had danced with him very briefly, with a cast of thousands, sort of wall-to-wall *Romeo and Juliets* at a theatre on the outskirts of Paris, about ten different casts from the Paris Opéra. He wanted some help to get them ready. Then I went back to assist him in something else, and he said, "Lil, what about teaching?" And I went, "Not here, for Christ' sake. They'll eat me for breakfast." And he said, "Yeah, come on," so I started there. It was very difficult, I found it terrifying, really, but he was wonderful because he'd come to all the classes and do them, and then I'd get a very considered critique after. Some of the dancers really liked it and some didn't, but the people that were the most difficult were the pianists, because they liked playing 3/4 [waltz time] all the time, and I didn't want that.

I needed twos and fours and threes because 3/4 makes everything so baggy. "But we *always* play 3/4 for ronds de jambe par terre." "No, not for me."

Experience is very helpful. I'm sure the qualities you need depend on what and who you're teaching. If you're going to teach students in a provincial school who just want a basic education, probably your requirements are different than somebody who's working at a school like Rambert that's mainly for dance and dance-related subjects. You've got kids that are very serious about it, you have to start giving them what they're going to need in later life, the building blocks, right away and very earnestly. For professionals, I think teachers need to be creative artists in their own right. They need to be highly intelligent, they have to be analytical, they have to have had experience, they need to be very special people. All too often they're rather mediocre, and it's hard for the people in the upper echelons of a company because you've got no one to help you. That was certainly the case at the Royal Ballet: there were no coaches. There was Gerd Larsen, who was an idiot, a sweet, sort of ditzy, totally useless lady. The only person that was in any way helpful was Brian Shaw, and he was a limited fellow, rather icy cold. There was no one. I think it would have been great if they'd had Moira Shearer and Pamela [May] in. I'd worked with them both in various things, they were fantastic. They'd had a lot of experience, they had a lot of warmth and humanity, and… they'd been there. Also, they were generous-spirited people, who were happy to help you on your way. They weren't going to push their thing on you but help you develop your own thing, they were very open like that. So often…Somes, who was such a horror, just wanted you to do it one way, absolutely rigid, ghastly, hideous soul-destroying stuff.

Coaching is teaching too nowadays, because so many dancers don't get a lot of early experience like we used to when we toured and did eight shows a week. They're not on the stage now very much at all, and as a result their stagecraft and know-how about what's important on the stage is terribly lacking. Also what's happening is that we just see the classroom on the stage. We go to a Brendel [piano] concert, and he transcends the notes on the page and it becomes music. We don't get this with dance. We get a whole bunch of people and we can still see all the notes, quite well performed in some cases but we don't go into…that music place. First of all they're not helped to use their imagination, they do not go through a creative process. They're told what to do, they're not encouraged to use their own intuition, their own knowledge. And worse than that, they're told by people who aren't artists anyway. I mean, I don't know everywhere, I've not been everywhere, but I think dancers don't dance as much anymore, so I imagine the problem is fairly universal.

I lost heart [with the classics] because I wasn't given any encouragement to do them until Rudolf came, and then no one wanted me to do them. I did them endlessly when I was a kid, all over the provinces. I've done more *Swan Lake*s than most ballerinas and *Beauty*s—I used to do three a week for months on end. And you rehearse by yourself, you do it all off your own bat. I wasn't given any help but I kept being told how lousy I was, and I'd been slaving away, so that's where the disheartening comes in. Then Rudolf comes along and says, "Let's try it my way." And [then] I had to beg for them. I didn't do them very much, but we did a lot of *Giselle*s together. But I think I only did one *Swan Lake* with him, and Kenneth didn't like me working with him so I was never allowed to do it again. And the *Beauty* I did with Rudolf...Natasha [Makarova] was pregnant, and I went and asked for it—I'd never done that in my life before. So we did three on the trot, and we had no dress rehearsal.

Now they do them all exactly the same. I don't think they're taught that there's any difference. When you see the adagio in *Giselle* and you can see their knickers, I mean, please! We see that in all the other [classics], and where's the beauty in this, where's the harmony, where's the taste? There's no taste at all, it's just unbelievable vulgarity. How are they allowed to do that? Who lets them do it? Who makes them think that that's great? I wouldn't go and look at them. Would you? I don't see any value in them for the dancers. Absolutely none. It's like thinking you can do the cancan. *Giselle*'s lasted because it's a wonderful story, and the music's really good as well. But I don't like the way it's performed anymore, I haven't seen a really, really good production of it for the longest time.

The other thing that's very hard in all these ballets, especially when you're [coaching] somebody who hasn't done them before, is the stamina. The condition you have to be in to do them is tops, and if you haven't been doing a lot of performing you have to find it in the rehearsal room, because otherwise you get on the stage and you don't know what's hit you. So you can help them through that, because it's quite hard finding the wherewithal to work yourself that hard so that you go on with...a tiger in your tank, a little bit to spare.

Oh, it's lovely coaching one's own roles. Because you know what the choreographer was looking for that you didn't, perhaps, necessarily realize yourself, you can tell them, "Look, he wanted this...I don't think I got that, but...Maybe you can do it." But again, in both the Ashton and the MacMillan things there's a lot of compromise involved now, ever diminishing the choreography. For one thing, I told you, Ashton used to make these floor plans. And his work is renowned for being very, very exhausting; you lose your breath because he wants you to use your body so much and also to travel these distances. Of course, this gets minimized and minimized, these concepts of space and movement; because they're so hard to do, they seem to get reduced and reduced and reduced. So you've got something that looks a bit like Ashton.

With MacMillan, they treat all his ballets like a Petipa ballet now. Well, he wanted them to be twentieth-century, not Romantic stories. He wanted them to be shocking, with a lot of sexual innuendo. And that's all gone. Also, his choreography was vertiginous, it was all off balance, and now it's like this, upright. You were falling, everything was...all the solos were falling, all the pas de deux, you were off balance all the time. And now they're all playing it safe on a straight axis.

I don't think these kids have...Not only don't they have a lot of performances, they don't have enormous rehearsal time. And then, like my experience, they probably don't have particularly good coaches. I don't know. We never did, but that might have changed. Well, *I* can't do it, I can't go in there and say, "I'm going to take this rehearsal." I have to be invited. That hasn't happened, and it won't either. With the MacMillan stuff, I refused to help with the *Sleeping Beauty* revival at ENB because I thought the production was such crap, and they were going to do it in six weeks, right after the holiday, right off the beach, and not let me tweak it around at all. I said to Deborah [MacMillan], "I can't work like that. For me it won't be interesting unless I can make some changes, because there are some bits of this ballet that don't look like Kenneth did it." For instance, there was some ghastly dénouement with the good and evil forces, the Lilac Fairy and Carabosse, that was so idiotic. Anyway, I looked at all the tapes, and I gave the *répétiteurs* my ideas on what they needed to watch out for. But I didn't want to be involved because it makes me heartsick. And I haven't been asked to do anything with the MacMillan people since. The same thing happened at the Royal Ballet because I criticized the director when we were putting on the Isadora dances [Ashton's *Five Brahms Waltzes in the Manner of Isadora Duncan*]. I haven't been asked back since then either.

There's too many people out there who say, Do this, Do that, and in fact, you have to work together with the person to find *their* way of fulfilling the vision of the choreographer. You don't say, "Do it like this because I did it"; you have to help them so that you actually re-create it. I know when I go about and do the Isadora dances I seem to meet with kindred spirits, but they're not allowed to work like that. It's all there, I just don't think it's ever brought out, and they love it…if you've got the right person. It's like anything: you don't go to a doctor that you don't get on with, you don't go to the shrink that you don't get along with. In a way it's the same with a coach: you might just not be on the same wavelength. Sometimes it's fear that makes them not receptive, people are frightened of change. It's very often fear and insecurity that make them a little bit unyielding. So you have to make them feel safe and willing to experiment, so that they find that it's not going to kill them to do something slightly differently and that it's actually quite fun. Often they have such a short time, and they're always being judged, onstage and in the rehearsal room too. So you've got to create a kind of *ambiance* where it's safe to fail, it's safe to fall over, it's safe to make a mistake, it doesn't matter, this is how we find where we're going. But you need time to do that, you need trust.

What interested me always, of course, was how to play around with everything. I think most creative people like doing that. You don't see that much now, and you don't see anyone taking risks either for the reasons I've just described, and I think that risk is one of the exciting things. They're too afraid to do it.

Only when I'm invited do I get involved. As I said, I've burned a lot of my bridges by upsetting the people who call the shots, so I don't do very much, to be honest. I think coaching would suit me very well. I enjoy it a lot. I've done it elsewhere [outside Britain], but it's usually with my repertoire. People these days don't think of asking me to do the classics.

I'm the wrong person to ask about the audience, because I was never ever aware of an audience being there. It wasn't *why* I was there. I never thought I was performing for an audience. I wasn't there to show myself—I was there to show the role. Obviously you draw on aspects of yourself, but it's not about you, it's about the role you're doing. So I don't think it was ever a cathartic experience in terms of my own self. That would be wallowing in egotism and the onanistic, and I wouldn't like that to happen, not my style.

One of my prides was the performances I did with Rudolf of *Sleeping Beauty*, because I was working against my nature and I did a good job. And the other moment I had of tremendous happiness was thinking, 'Well, I've managed to do that, and it's the last time I'll be doing it.' That was a performance of Act III *Anastasia* at the Met with ENB, and the happiness was to have pulled it off. I was trying to fulfill an idea in a certain circumstance, and frankly I didn't care if the audience liked it or not. It wasn't a concern. But when you're not a natural show-off, as it were, it's very brave—for a lot of people, I'm not alone in this—to be in that position of being scrutinized so closely and exposed when that's your least favorite thing. It's an act of bravery every time. Some people take naturally to the limelight and they respond to it in a marvelous way. I just wasn't one of those people.

I think there's been, both politically and in other ways, an attempt to popularize dance so that it's amenable, easily approachable, by Joe Public. But I don't think that they do it the right way, because you don't have to talk down. You show them something that's easily accessible and lead them into how [other] things work. In between there's *Strictly Come Dancing*, there's all the musicals with marvelous dancing, there's tap dancing, there's the wonderful acrobats, there's all those other popular things. It doesn't mean ballet has to do the same—it should just be itself. Otherwise it becomes a banality. It's not the real thing and it's all really rather absurd.

I don't often go and see ballet, frankly. Unless they start doing more new stuff, I hope it dies a death, because the way it is right now it's not worth looking at. There's no intellectual anything going into it. It's all just, Let's put the show on we put on last year, but we have to cut six hours off the rehearsal time. So...like, cut the cloaks.

When I stopped dancing I went to the London School of Psychotherapy, because I have mental health problems myself and

I wanted to find more out about it. I thought that there's very little help for dancers in this area and a lot of them suffer from psychological problems, and I also thought it would help my work. So I did a two-year course; I didn't want to become a psychotherapist. I use what I learned all the time, especially in the rehearsal room. The fear and the fear of change I was talking about are key to a lot of psychological problems and key to whether you can be creative or not. The creative instinct is strong in most people, and it's very satisfactory when you can use it, it gives you great pleasure.

There was one psychologist who had a theory of creativity which I just adored. He's an American called Carl Rogers. He's now dead, but he developed a whole school of counseling and psychotherapy called the humanistic school, and his theory of creativity or "towards a theory of creativity"...for me it was like a handbook for any artistic institution, because it makes immediate sense. Absolutely basic to the creative experience is to be in a place where you can make mistakes, try all kinds of things out, in a non-judgmental *ambiance* where you're working together to find something. It doesn't matter if you make an ass of yourself on the way, and it can be quite fun. I use it all the time, and it works fabulously. You get performances from people, you encourage them to pull out the stuff from themselves, and they have a wonderful experience.

A couple of years ago perhaps, Ghislaine [Thesmar, then a *répétiteur* for the Paris Opéra Ballet] said things have changed at the Paris Opéra, and in Denmark things have slipped horribly badly, evidently. It's this sort of corporate thing. What we all think is that the people at the top of the ballet roster, who direct these companies, are chosen by people who know nothing about it or very little. They're chosen by boards and the boards don't know anything about ballet, they don't understand how it works. They want it to be neat and tidy, so they get on the whole people who are probably safe and probably pretty mediocre, who then surround themselves with safe and mediocre people. Nikolaj [Hübbe, director of the Royal Danish Ballet] is going to have trouble because he's working with a built-in structure. Again, like Munich, they won't want to change. And here, the same. The Royal Ballet doesn't even do an hour and a half class. They never have. They've always done an hour and a quarter. That's why no one can do grand allegro, because they don't have time to get there in class. Also, everyone's left by then, most of them won't be there for the jumps. And also, because the class is short, they don't have enough tendus battements to start with. They're weak, they're not in condition. Nikolaj's saying the same about the Danes, that they have no condition at all.

It's just so sad. I mean, it's so unjoyful. It's such a pity, because there are many gifted people out there. They're all around somewhere, and it just seems so wasteful that the sort of sacred youth must be brought up but there's no attempt to use the older artists' qualities. They might not have the stamina they once did, but most of them have the flexibility and the artistry and the experience to carry off something really quite marvelous. There's no attempt made ever to try and lengthen their careers or lead them on to another one. They don't start teaching in the company or start taking rehearsals while they're still dancing...I don't know why, lack of imagination basically. If you're in the company already dancing, why can't you help some younger dancers learn something? It doesn't have to be one of your roles, it could be the Fairies' dances in *Sleeping Beauty*. Or why can't you take some rehearsals with some of the youngsters? Well, there aren't any older artists now. They get rid of everybody so young. It is, actually, a waste of resource. A misuse of a great resource...or no use.

London
October 2008

Antoinette Sibley

Antoinette Sibley (b. Bromley, England, 1939) spent five years studying ballet, tap and musical comedy dancing at the Arts Educational School before entering the Royal Ballet School in 1949. The first British ballerina to pass straight through the school, she graduated into the corps of the Royal Ballet in 1956, advanced to soloist in 1959—when she danced her first *Swan Lake* at Covent Garden on 12 hours' notice—and attained the rank of principal the following year. Refined, elegant and supremely musical, she took naturally to the classical repertory and created 12 notable roles, including Titania in Ashton's *The Dream* (1964) and the title part in MacMillan's *Manon* (1974). The former work inaugurated her extraordinary partnership with Anthony Dowell, which continued until her initial retirement in 1979 and resumed two years later, when she returned to the company for a further ten years of performing.

§§§

From 1991, the year she left the stage for good, until 2012, Sibley served as president of the Royal Academy of Dance, under whose auspices she established the Fonteyn Nureyev Young Dancers Competition in 2005. Having spent her entire life within the Royal Ballet, she remained involved with it as a member of the ballet board from 1992 to 1998, a governor of the Royal Ballet companies from 2000 to 2005, and an occasional coach of the classics and of the roles she originated, particularly in the Ashton repertory. She has also coached these roles for English National Ballet.

When I was writing a book about her in the 1980s, I visited her regularly at home, where we met again this time after considerable juggling to find an opening in her schedule. She arrived in her kitchen carrying her diary and a stack of files, which she spread out between us for reference.

§§§

One thing led to another. I mean, I had never proposed to go back. I had done my career and I now had my daughter, my baby, and it was idyllic. Then Anthony rang me about this one-parent family gala, which was in his honor, and therefore, he sweetly said, I must appear in it and what would we do? So I said, "Well, of course I haven't danced for..." however long it was...a year, I don't know, for me it was finished. Sort of jokingly I said, "Obviously I can't dance, so I'll read a poem." He said, "That's fine," and I left it at that.

Then a wee while after that, I found I was pregnant again. So I rang him with the joyous news, and he said, "What about my gala?" to which I replied, "That's all right, I'll read my poem in a tent dress." I didn't think much more about it, but I clearly was somewhere slotted in on the program. Then my son came two months early, so I said to Anthony, "Obviously it's good news in a way, because I won't need a tent dress." And he said, "By the way, Ashton's going to organize this pas de deux for us." So I went, "How am I going to do a pas de deux after not dancing?" So he said, "He's going to write it especially. You'll be in little bootees. It's a little Edwardian number about a poem called *Soupirs*, and we'll just be around a bench."

Then, as the time was coming nearer, I'd been so weighed back with my weight carrying this child that I thought, 'I'll just go and do a barre or two to get my weight forward again, so when I walk on the stage I'm not like some weird mama.' So I started doing these little barres and pretty soon found that actually I was happier on pointe rather than half-pointe because that kept making my calves ache. And so although we started the rehearsals in these little shoes, by the end I found I'd got such bad calves that I got rid of the shoes and did it on pointe, and it was a big success. What then happened was that Ashton and Anthony said, "This has been such a big success, would you repeat it?" I don't know now whether it was in New York or in London, it was for some big do, so I went, "Yes, fine, I'd love to." And that again was going to be the end of the story as far as I was concerned. I never, *ever* thought…I mean, I've now got my second baby, so was I likely to go back and work?

Anyway, we did do that, and following that very quickly [Robert] Helpmann said to me—see, it's all these wonderful personalities—Helpmann said, "Well, if you could do that, you can certainly go to New York and do Ophelia [in his *Hamlet*]. She's not even on pointe." I said, "That would be lovely," because New York was always my favorite place. So I did New York, then we had to repeat it in London because we'd danced it in New York, and then came up the fiftieth anniversary of the company, and Ashton said "You've absolutely *got* to do the *Dream* pas de deux." Well, Anthony couldn't do it, he was injured by then anyway, and I *certainly* couldn't do it. That's quite a different thing to *Soupirs*. I could *not* get up and hop on pointe and jump around and be light and all this, and it's eight minutes long. There was no way.

So we both simply put our heels in, we said, "We'll repeat *Soupirs* or repeat Ophelia going mad, but we absolutely cannot do that." But they went on and on, and Ashton started getting really upset. He said, "I don't care if you do it in galoshes." We've both got those words written down, so whatever anybody says, we say, "Fred said, 'You can do it in your galoshes.'" So of course we did do it, for Michael [Somes] and for Ashton, and we actually had to cut out some of Anthony's huge jumps and I just couldn't do the hops on pointe. We changed four steps which he wanted us to do, he would rather have us on than not. And then, that was it, that was the end.

You see, these were all incidental things being dropped in my lap. Ashton's very persuasive, and Somes is and so is Helpmann, and it was for the company, it was the fiftieth anniversary. And once I could do the *Dream* pas de deux, I'd got an awful lot under my belt, because it's really tough. So I don't know what came up next, but when I had done whatever that was, I realized, well, I was…hooked. I only did my rep. I never did a classic again. I did classical things, I did *Cinderella*, and Fred wanted me to do *Scènes de Ballet*, which, funnily enough, although it's killing, always came naturally for me. I think it was probably after a *Scènes de Ballet* that I made a final decision to continue. It wasn't meant to happen, it never really was talked about. It was just one thing, then you do the whole *Dream*, and then it's "Can you do…?" and it's *Cinderella*, a three-act ballet. So things were landing in my lap that were my own ballets, if you know what I mean, and came naturally to me. I wasn't forcing my body into something I found impossible.

All this time I was having opportunities as well, apart from working with Anthony all the time. Misha [Baryshnikov] was very much around—we had made the film [*The Turning Point*] and we very much wanted to do something together. He again was one of these people who said, "Now you're back, would you do…?" so I did *Month in the Country* with Misha and *Raymonda*s and things with Rudolf [Nureyev]. It was really these people, if I think about it, but I didn't think about it because it just was topsy-turvy. Nothing was actually planned—it just happened that every time an Ashton ballet came up, my name was down there [on the cast sheet].

And also, very important to all of this was Madame [Shulamith] Messerer. She was teaching us. She was an amazing teacher, and after I did that first gala, she said, "You've got to keep dancing. You've got such a lot there, you can't give up now. I can give you ten more years." So I did class with her every day, and in fact I *did* have ten years. It was a joke at the time, we laughed, but on looking back…It was very much my rep, very much my partners, even if I hadn't danced a lot with them it was wonderful to have the opportunity to explore more.

Then, after doing these wonderful ten years, all my various partners started doing less and less. Rudolf by now was hardly doing anything, just a few things with the Paris Opéra, Misha wasn't doing a lot of classical things anymore, Anthony was cutting down. I'd already started working with Stephen Jefferies and with Wayne Eagling, which was very nice in that I'd never worked with them before. I was going around the world doing a gala here, a gala there, but my partners were starting to go. And as it was, I arranged all my time and rehearsals around my children—whenever I wasn't working, I was with my family. So of course when things got less, I got more of the family. I was just as busy, but I was busy with them as opposed to dancing.

What made the final break…I don't know why, I'd made the decision that I would stop after the *Month in the Country*. *Dream* wouldn't come up again in the rep for two or three years, so I couldn't end on that, so *Month in the Country* seemed a very good option. So I did my last one in London and I never said anything to anybody, except obviously Anthony knew, my husband in the ballet, Derek Rencher, knew, and my real husband knew. Nobody else knew because I didn't want a brouhaha. I did not want all those things being thrown, balloons and paper chucked and all these speeches, I couldn't face one of those big ordeals. So I thought the best thing was…It was coming into New York—I'd always intended to finish in New York—and I would just announce it on the day. A month before we were due to go, the tour was cancelled, so my career came to an end with the tablecloth sort of pulled away. In fact, I had finished already and I didn't even know it.

But, oh god, I'm always wanting to do nothing. I am the biggest person wanting to do nothing in the world. I'd been a vice-president of the RAD for a wee while, I mean, as people die they put in new vice-presidents, but there was no work entailed. It was just they wanted, I suppose, to have ballerinas…I was a name on the letterhead, I didn't really do anything. Oh, no, I might very well have helped David Wall, if this was the time he was the chief executive, because I certainly did do some judging for him for the Adeline Genée [International Ballet Competition], as it was called then, it's now called the Genée. Maybe I'd started doing that, but it was only three or four days.

Then Margot [Fonteyn] died. Margot died in 1991, and that's when…I don't know why [the RAD] asked me [to replace her], but they did. I think they wanted me because I was a vice-president and the next step, I suppose, is president, and maybe I was a suitable age. I'd been doing these Adeline Genées, I knew Ivor Guest, who was at that point the chairman [of the executive committee], and I knew David Wall, I knew them all, but it was just because Margot died. And I thought, 'Well, Margot did it from a distance, so it can't be that involving.' You know, Margot was in Panama, so the last ten years of her life she wasn't coming forward and back like she had all her life. So I probably thought that I could go to one meeting here and one meeting there and that would be that. But what I didn't realize was that the Academy was going through a difficult period in every respect, and I naturally wanted to know what was happening. So I started going to all these meetings, the artistic, the educational, the executive, the financial side. My husband came in to help them deal with the financial situation. David Wall got everybody that he could to help.

What was different for me was that as a dancer, even for the ten years I came back, everything was really about my dancing and my working with these incredible people. I was utterly, utterly spoiled all my life and I knew it, from Madame Karsavina right through to all the choreographers...obviously Ashton and MacMillan and Jerry Robbins...I mean, I chuck these names out, but each single one is magic. And I suppose in a way I thought, 'Now I'm dealing with children who are learning to dance, and it's a worldwide organization. It must be a good thing to help the young ones, just starting up.' It was new to me to help them and see how they get on. I didn't teach, I wasn't a teacher and I didn't want to be a teacher, but I thought in this respect I would be in touch with ballet with the young, coming into it and going through it and then reaching the stage.

When I was a child, we just had the 1, 2, 3, 4, 5 and elementary, intermediate, advanced [levels of the RAD syllabus]; I used to do [that syllabus] at Arts Educational. Then when I went to the Royal Ballet School we did it once a week like we did Cecchetti [syllabus] once a week, and the rest of the time we did de Valois' syllabus. So I had taken some [RAD] exams, not all of them, I think we stopped at elementary at the Royal Ballet School. But I was also doing tap exams, we were doing exams all the time, it was just one of those things that you had to do at the end of every term or every year. So I had done some of the syllabus, and when I came upon it now, they wanted to enlarge it. Instead of doing up to Grade 5 and [then] elementary, intermediate, advanced, they were going to put in [Grades] 6, 7 and 8, and a lot of our artistic committee were going to be setting these new levels. So they said, "Why don't you create a solo for this age group?" as part of the exam. When I say a solo, it was just a little sequence. So I did do two little sequences for the exam of Grade 6 and 7, and it was the first time I'd ever put step to step. I thought it was quite sweet, actually; I liked that.

I did also bring in two big things for the Academy. One, I was able to bring back the mime. [Irina] Baronova and Karsavina were both very important to us at the Academy at various times, and one or both did [teach] a mime class as well. It was part of the culture of our dancing and our ethics at the Academy. The importance of it just cannot be lost, and I could see that mime *was* getting lost in so many companies worldwide. It was being chopped off, so I really, really wanted to do a video on mime, and the Academy supported me with it because it was so important. [The critic] Clement Crisp did the chat on it and wonderful dancers were involved, all the great mime artists from our company. Anthony did the *Lac* mime scene with me, we had Monica [Mason], we had Deanne Bergsma, Johan Kobborg, Alina [Cojocaru], Pamela May and Barbara Fewster, absolutely everyone was involved. It was on the importance of mime and where it came from, where it goes to, and how vital it is to ballet. "A historical document" you could call it—sounds quite highfaluting.

And the other thing...Of course we had no money at the Academy, it's always difficult, but I started this competition, the Fonteyn Nureyev competition. Oh, the Genée is quite different. Our final exam is the Genée. This is the last thing they do before they become professional. We don't have anybody doing this exam who's already in a company and earning their money. It's not a free-for-all for anyone to come and join. This is for students. For everybody who does our syllabus from the age of four or whenever they start, this is the big prize. And now—it's a new thing—we do [the Genée] in different countries which have our syllabus all over the world. We started out with Australia, where people were literally queuing around [the building] trying to get tickets. We took it to Hong Kong, where it was sold out six months in advance, and that's not just the Genée; we also do some classes, and sometimes I do a masterclass. We also have our artistic director, Lynn Wallis, talking about the syllabus or showing different parts of it. So it's three or four days when we go to these places, and for the students it's the peak of their study. The whole thing's on the stage, so it's the final thing before they go into a company where they're going to be on the stage all their life.

We went to Athens for the Olympic Games, and then it was Toronto this year, which was fantastic, the front page of the newspaper was all about us. In this country, it's come to slopping down to watch the television or whatever they do. There isn't the excitement or wonder...Nobody desires or needs to travel anywhere to do *anything* nowadays. All over the world, they do. That's why we took [the Genée] from England. We do still bring it back but not every year like we used to. We do it now every other year or every third year. But everywhere else it's just incredible how interested they all are; there's real fascination and excitement about it.

I did one other competition, in New York. What I didn't like about it, having come from my world, is that...They're not as fair as the way we do it, let's put it that way. We only have three judges, so there's no whispering and trying to get this one in that we like or that one in that we like. We have one other judge who joins us for the semi-finals, so there are only four of us in the whole thing, and it's very fair, because we can't hide anything. There's no numbers that are put in a box [as scores]. We just talk it out between us. There is no way that anybody could get past us or through us or 'round us—it's a very open competition.

Now, Fonteyn Nureyev...Actually, it's the Fonteyn Nureyev Young Dancers Competition, and it takes place every other year in England. The reason I did something here was they did some research to discover how many people take the exams, and they found that between the age of 10 and 12 the droppage was colossal. I mean, something like sixty percent were dropping out of the RAD, not taking our exams, i.e., they're not going on up to become dancers or teachers, that's where they're stopping. This was shocking, and I realized why [it was happening] because I remembered myself when I was that age. Unless you have a chance to perform...If your exams are all working towards doing something on the stage, that shows you that all these awfully boring classes that one does every day have got an end in view, and the end in view is to be on the stage, to use that music, to use the steps, to portray something. That's what it's all about, and unless you get that into your bloodstream as a teenager, of course you're going to give up. Why would you want to go on seeing yourself in the mirror looking ghastly all the time [when] all your friends are going out with boys and doing lovely things? It's just not on. You need something which really is part of the theatre. The wanting to be on the stage, in the theatre, that's the way to hook you with ballet, because ballet's just so hard. I mean, why would anybody do ballet? It's much harder than acting...physically it's like being an athlete. It's constant, every day work, constantly seeing yourself looking awful, nothing is ever perfect. *Always* something is going wrong, you can't help it.

There are very few British principals in the [Royal Ballet] company, and at that time I think there were even less. There have never been a huge number, because we used to have lots of Commonwealth ballerinas and danseurs nobles. So my worry is that if all our people, the British people, were stopping their exams...If one can prevent them from dropping out, you've got a hope at least that the ones who stay will be good at it and that they also will want to get on the stage. So passing this jolly thing will keep them going for those few years until they can *go* on the stage. That was my main aim, because…well, it was just obvious. If the theatre was very much part of their ballet lessons, they had something to work to, something to want to do. Funnily enough, *not* in the way that I did, because I was at the Royal Ballet School and I didn't go on the stage 'til I was 16 or 17, as a swan. I did not have any of this. But I think to go to the Royal Ballet School at all you had to want to be doing it, you had to need to be doing it. First of all, to get in…you're not from the bottom of the pot. They only take the crème de la crème. And just to be there all the time…We were working then towards a summer school that de Valois would give every year for teachers from all over the world. Although it wasn't like acting or even doing any dances, it was with de Valois and you were doing her syllabus in front of all these teachers. So in a way it was a performance, and you were working to get to it, and obviously your end in view was to get into a company. I think it's far more diffused with the RAD. By the time you're ten, eleven, twelve, you're doing tap classes, ballroom classes, all sorts of other classes as well. The students all around the country are not necessarily just doing RAD [ballet], they've got other classes going on around them.

I was also on the ballet board of the opera house, I don't know from when, and now I am the vice-chairman of the governors. I suppose we talk about the various problems that come up…It's not just the Royal Ballet company, you see. Even when I was on the Royal Ballet board, it was always about the Birmingham Royal Ballet, our company, and White Lodge, the school—there were always the three. It was important that there was a gathering of people who could discuss the various problems that arose and help to iron them out with the directors. Monica [Mason, director of the Royal Ballet] comes to our meetings, Gailene [Stock, director of the Royal Ballet School] comes to our meetings, David Bintley [director of Birmingham Royal Ballet], and they report what's happening and what's going wrong one way or another, and hopefully we can help. It's an advisory committee. We can't take any world-shattering decisions, but I've been in the organization since I was nine years old. So from then to…what am I now?…nearly 70, I've learnt…I've *had* to learn…You do pick up quite a bit, and you can report on how it worked with you or how you've seen it not work with others and maybe it's a good idea to do this or to do that. At least it's good advice from someone who's been connected with it right the way through. You can't help but have something rubbed off on you, and it's really important that you can pass this on. It doesn't have to be picked up if they don't want to, but at least you've been there. I'm just reporting what I have learnt through my years, if it's helpful.

Now, coaching is my fulfillment. I get as much or almost as much fulfillment out of that as I did when I danced. Maybe "almost as much" rather than "as much," but it's more than any of these other things that I've talked about. Although really interesting, I find all of those things quite a lot of work, and to pass on movement and all I've learnt through moving to music and the drama of it all...that's where my natural personality lies.

I started off in a very mild way, not meaning to go anywhere, just because I adored working with Viviana Durante and she happened to be in lots of ballets with me. I shouldn't say "working with her," it wasn't as structured as that. But we were great friends, I adored her work, and we often were playing against each other. So if I saw her at the back of a class trying to do a pirouette or something, it would suddenly occur to me that if she used the left arm it might help. Or when she did her little solo in *Month in the Country* I might suggest something, purely as a friend, as an older friend, and we got on really well. I didn't help anybody else, other than people I danced with, like Anthony. You refine things, naturally, but that's just a colleague helping a colleague, and this is what it was with Viviana, a colleague helping a colleague.

You see, when I did split [from dancing], I didn't want anything else to do with it. I was going to be with my children and all that, the RAD hadn't come up. And Anthony rang me, he was then the director of the company, and he said he was bringing back *Scènes de Ballet*, and of course *Scènes de Ballet* is one of my greatest loves. I think it's one of the greatest ballets ever written, and I was fortunate to do it for 25 years, all the way through 'til I was nearly 50, and Ashton had the confidence in me or wanted me or needed me to do it, I don't know. So Anthony said, "You'll have to come and help teach it—wear your galoshes—because you've had Fred all that time giving you all these corrections. They must be inside you, you can help." And he said, "Viviana's going to do it for the first time." So the two things together, Ashton's *Scènes de Ballet*—obviously he'd given *me* so much, it was only right that I should pass it on— and Viviana going to do it. Perfect. Then I started rehearsing her in general, in *Giselle* and *Swan Lake*.

That's how it started and it literally went on from there, with hundreds of other dancers. I've taught *Manon* and *Dream* to Cojocaru, I helped [Tamara] Rojo with a bit of *Manon*, Sarah Lamb, [Mara] Galeazzi, [Alessandra] Ansanelli *Sleeping Beauty*. And [Federico] Bonelli, of course Kobborg, all the people who work *with* them, because in the Ashton ballets like *Daphnis and Chloe* and in *Manon*, the men are part of it too. I did *Swan Lake* and *Giselle* with these people who I worked with a lot. I did all the *Sleeping Beautys*, and when Anthony's *Sleeping Beauty* came in, I helped Darcey [Bussell]. For one wee period, Anthony and I helped Sylvie [Guillem], even Sylvie, for *Afternoon of a Faun*. Because Jerry was in Paris and he was going to come over and finish it, he said, Wouldn't it be good if Anthony and I helped her and that Hungarian [Zoltán Solymosi], very handsome, very temperamental, who she was dancing with. In the end, they didn't do it, because unfortunately it was cancelled.

All I go back to is Kenneth or Fred or Jerry, to what I was taught by them, the different things they were looking for and what they really, really wanted. I can't speak for Petipa, obviously. I would never want anyone to do anything—this is an absolute ground rule—like *I* did it, because my personality is absolutely nothing like any of these people I coach, not like Cojocaru, not like Darcey or anybody. They've all got their own personalities. All I can do is do what Ashton and MacMillan and all these other people gave to me. There are certain steps that they would go on and on about, even for 25 years.

Well, in *Manon*, in the solo in the second act, there's a step where I've got my back to the audience and all I do is a jump, échappé, and then I just bring my leg in onto the pointe. But over, over and over Kenneth said that I wasn't jumping high enough in the échappé. To me, it was in the middle of the solo and one's quite tired at that point, and I always used to do it and make a lot of bringing in the foot to the pointe. He was insistent about this échappé—it had to be higher, so that my feet were pointed *off* the floor, that's the position he wanted to see. Every time I did it, every time he repeated this. And now I see what he means, because when the dancers come to it, they're doing exactly what I did, a little échappé. Because you're tired, you don't want to jump up, you've got your back to the audience, you don't think anybody's noticing how high it is. But you notice amazingly, not so much in the new dress that Agnes [Oaks] wore [in the English National Ballet production] but in that original black lace dress you really notice those pink tights and pink shoes, I mean, you zoom in. And it does look dreadful if you don't actually get in the air.

There were things they definitely wanted; even if it was difficult to do, that's what they saw, and it wasn't anything to do with the way you interpret. Tudor, for instance, who used to take us in *Lilac Garden*...He kept stopping us and saying, "What are you thinking?" He needed you to think thoughts, and it showed through your eyes if you weren't thinking. With Ashton, as we all know, it's épaulement and the body, moving the body, and the eyes, use the eyes. In certain ballets, like *Scènes de Ballet*, you'd get in a position and he'd *hoick* you into it, so it clearly stays with you. It felt exaggerated, but you can see so clearly how right they were to ask for these things, which didn't feel that important to you, perhaps, when you were doing it.

So it's a joy for me to do it, and within this last year I've had the most amazing time. I was putting on *Daphnis and Chloe* with Anthony with the Birmingham company. Then I had the English National Ballet for *Manon*, four different couples, all those pas de deux, and I've seen darling Agnes and Thomas [Edur] do it now, and they were absolutely wonderful and getting back a whole lot of the little innuendos that sometimes can get lost. They're all wonderfully receptive. I haven't come across anyone who hasn't been avid for these little details and little timings and little ways. That's what one gets back—they're just so thrilled.

They're very, very athletic nowadays, much more so than we were, and they can get into these extraordinary positions because they're so, so loose. This is another use of the body—we didn't do *those* things. We did maybe as exhausting things, with the shoulders and the body, using every bit of your body, but we didn't have the huge looseness of the limbs, the legs that can go over more than 180 degrees. It wasn't called for, we weren't asked to do that, but most of their ballets require it; so many of them are in overall tights. I was mainly in tutus or in dresses.

But, you see, in *Beauty* or *Lac* you only have the time of the music to get to a certain position, so you can't...Whether you're doing a fish dive or whatever, the steps are the steps. Of course you can get your leg a bit higher in the fish dive, but then what you lose is the wonderful line that Anthony and I had. You can equally do it with the legs going over more so it's like a U, but you've only got the same amount of music. So you are trapped, in a way, by the

steps and the music, and if you go and change the music...We, my
generation, try and keep what the choreographer intended for the
music. I find that a lot of the Manons like to do the [second-act]
solo slower now, because it's easier to do it slower, it's not so tiring.
I think it's a mistake...and I'm not Kenneth, Kenneth might like it
with that person interpreting it that way. But my point of view is
that what comes later, with all the men carrying you and passing
you over their heads, that *is* slow. So the solo that he set on me—he
actually did it himself, marvelously—was faster, and you've got the
contrast. But you are exhausted—good job they are carrying one,
absolutely.

What I loved about dancing was I just adore moving my body to
music, and the choreographers that I worked with, my goodness,
how they did move the body to music. Exploring with these wonderful steps that you were given is very athletic, and you get quite a
thrill physically. Something like *Ballet Imperial* is an absolute killer
and it's so, so, so difficult, but you get what a long-distance runner
must get. You are exhausted and you've used every inch of your
body to do these impossible things, and when you've done it...I
can't tell you...You just feel a hundred percent. It's a great, high
feeling of life. I can't compare it with drinking or anything—it's an
elixir, it's a real achievement. Just as it is, funnily enough, if you're
doing an acting ballet, because you use your whole personality [in]
the way you move and the way you react to steps and movement
and different people, but this time you are a person, whether it's
Cinderella or it's Manon. I was so lucky in my life, I had so many
yummy, yummy roles with so many wonderful creators. To be in
that room, working on a ballet with those great creators, has to
have been almost as great as when you do the performance and get
the comeback from the audience. That's what I'm hoping to pass
on. I can never be that person, but I am a second degree or a third
degree of that person.

Of course I never saw the ballets when I was in them, and
I was in them for so long. So I don't really know if they've
changed. They've got wonderful choreologists, particularly for
MacMillan's work, and I would think they learn quite a bit from
video. Everything helps, you use whatever you can to help you.
But I think it's quite useful to have...For instance, it was wonderful when Pamela May would come in and show us a few of the
things from *Symphonic Variations*. She was there when Ashton
put it on [originally], and the way she held her head and the way

she got into some of these positions, you have a picture of it and you can learn from that wonderfully. [Lubov] Tchernicheva and [Serge] Grigoriev taught us *Sylphides* and *Petrouchka*, so all that's from the horse's mouth.

I think also…I don't mean, as I said, to put one's own way of doing it onto somebody. I don't think that's correct at all, because they look so different from you, they dance so differently. Some have got big jumps that you want to use more—I didn't have a big jump. But when I've been rehearsed by somebody who's done a role for a long time, I find there just is something extra that I'm interested in. I don't mean you can't write everything down, but there's always a place for the people who've done these things, and I hope that the Vivianas and all these people who I've helped will remember some of the things to pass on again. I hope that's how it goes. I hope it doesn't all become just picking up a book and doing it or just watching a video, because that's not like somebody telling you, "Twist your shoulder. Bend over more," and actually pushing you into positions.

I had Karsavina, and I will *never* forget seeing Karsavina do the mime scene from *Giselle*, the mime scene from *Swan Lake*. This was private, in a studio. I can't remember how we got her…Oh, I know exactly what it was, it was for the classical ballet book [*Classical Ballet: The Flow of Movement*]. I was working with her all the time [on that], and one day I did ask her if she could just help me with a bit of the mime from *Swan Lake* and *Giselle*. She didn't think about it—she just did it. I don't know what age she was, but there was something so touching and amazing…She was just minute as well, and these eyes! One had heard Fred go on about her, you'd heard Margot and Michael…Michael was in love with her…all these people going on and on and on about "You've got to use your eyes. Think of Karsavina." Well, you can't think that until you see somebody do it, and when you see them…

I don't compare myself…I hasten to add immediately that I don't put myself on this level. All I know is there is something about somebody who's done it…well, as she did it, to such a high degree. I don't say I did that, but because of the connection with Ashton or MacMillan or somebody who *is* on that degree…You're a conduit, anyway.

I don't know whether the most exciting thing of all was working in the studio with the choreographer, because it was so private, or being so public, out there on the stage, being the person, becoming the person. I don't know which was the most satisfying of those two—I can't judge that, because they were both equal in fulfillment. And then on the next step would come passing it on.

I'm most proud of my children probably. But I put "probably" because obviously I'm proud of where I got to and Anthony and my whole career. I mean, how lucky can you be? How lucky to have work to come back to. How lucky to have a second bite of the apple. For me, the [final] ten years were more important than all those other years. I was a much better artist, I understood, I could get more from people, I could ask more questions, I wasn't so nervous, so worried...I was on top of the game in a way. And I had more opportunity, I danced more often. The ballets were not more of a challenge when I was older, no, *less* of a challenge, because I had the groundwork. Between 40 and 50...You have time to reflect, and because you've got more stage knowledge, because you're much older and you've done so much, you can put it into action much more. When I came back and I didn't do the classical ballets, I had more confidence for all these other things, not that I was going to do them brilliantly or anything like that, more confidence in what I wanted to achieve.

Maybe I'm being over-optimistic, but I can't imagine that ballet would ever go out. Why would it? If you think of what it's giving people, what the audiences get—forget the dancers and whatever it does for them—it is an unbelievable art. I'm not there every night but I go frequently, and I get the same thing that I get from going to the opera. I am completely taken out of myself. All the things that have been going on and you can't solve and you can't sort out, you go and you sit and the curtains open...it completely takes you out of your realistic situation in life, and I don't think that's ever going to die. However bad things get, people need it. Look how they need it—look how many companies we've got now. If you think back to when Madam [de Valois] started and Rambert started or even in my day, in the early career, and now we've got the Spanish dancers and the Brazilians, I'm looking at them all over the world, and it is so exciting and it gives back so much to the people. I don't think you're going to lose an art that combines the top music, the top acting, the top dancing, the top theatre. It's all in one, it all happens together. I don't think you could live...I don't imagine that civilizations would go on and not have something of that ilk.

As you can see from all of this, my life's been a jumble. Nothing has been programed, or if it has, it's immediately been stopped and changed. I don't really make plans. Right now Anthony and I are working on *The Dream* for the Royal Ballet School performance. At the moment we're just teaching the steps. Anthony's in charge of the whole thing, and I'm doing my bits. And I've got certain things that I'll set in the diary, like tomorrow I've got the governors meeting. And then, of course, things just come up. People say, "Oh, could you do this?" or "Could you do that?" and I go, "Yes, I'd love to."

I think it works out perfectly well actually, in my kind of muddled life. I'm always promising myself various things, that I'll read this or I'll tidy up that. I long to be able to do different things as well, I mean, I never go to museums, I never do half the things that one would also like. So I'm happy with how things are, that they come up and I do them.

London
January 2009

Monica Mason

Monica Mason (b. Johannesburg, South Africa, 1941) began her ballet training in South Africa and continued it in London, from the age of 14, with Nesta Brooking and at the Royal Ballet School. Having joined the Royal Ballet in 1958, she created the pivotal role of the Chosen Maiden in Kenneth MacMillan's *The Rite of Spring* (1962) while still a member of the corps de ballet. Advancing to soloist the following year and to principal in 1968, she acquired an enormous repertory that ranged from *Swan Lake* to *Dances at a Gathering*, displaying a particular flair for drama and comedy in such works as *Song of the Earth*, *Checkmate* and *Les Biches*. Leaving classical roles behind, she continued to appear in mime parts and to create new roles for MacMillan, David Bintley and William Tuckett. She gave her last performance at Covent Garden, as Carabosse, in 1997.

§§§

Within a year of our first conversation, Monica Mason began the gradual ascent to her position as director of the Royal Ballet. In 1980 she became Kenneth MacMillan's assistant, a role that developed four years later into that of principal *répétiteur* to the company. After four years as assistant to the director Anthony Dowell, in 1991 she was named the company's assistant director and promoted in 2002 to director, the post she retained until 2012. Thirty years ago, we talked in a coffee shop in Virginia while the Royal Ballet was on tour in America. She met me this time in her office in the Royal Opera House, not once but twice, cutting short her remarks one day to conduct a rehearsal and resuming our discussion several days later as if no time had intervened.

§§§

I was really bitten by the theatre bug and always loved being in the theatre and especially being a member of this company. I started out being astonished to be taken into the company when I *was* taken in, because...Towards the end of my first year at the school, I was told that I'd got a place in the [Sadler's Wells] Opera Ballet for what would be my second year. And suddenly, instead of going to the opera ballet and staying in the school I was told that I was going to join the main company. It was total astonishment, because I'd never danced with the company. I'd not been a swan, all I'd done was walk on as a supposedly aristocratic young lady in *Petrouchka*.

I couldn't believe that I was on the stage at the opera house and that I was in the same theatre as Maria Callas and Tito Gobbi. We kept absolutely quiet in the corridors when Callas was in the theatre, no one was allowed to go down the back stairs making a single sound, because you were back of Number 5 dressing room, which was Callas's dressing room. So when you've come 6,000 miles and suddenly you're *in* it...it takes a huge adjustment. My first rehearsal was *Ondine*, which was about to première. And of course Frederick Ashton was in the studio, and later on that afternoon Margot Fonteyn came in the studio. And very soon after that, Kenneth MacMillan was doing his big stage version of *Danses Concertantes*, and I became involved with that straightaway.

I don't think the love of dancing and the amazement at finding myself here ever left me. So when it came to the end of my career and I was going to have to stop...I went for an audition at the BBC to present an arts program for television, and I did the most awful audition. They said to me, "Could you try and modulate the tone of your voice? It's a little bit same-y all the time." The very next morning I was in the canteen and Kenneth came in, and he said, "Oh, hello, Miss Mason. I haven't seen you for a few days. What have you been up to?" just casual. So I said, "Last night I went for an audition at the BBC." And he said, "But you're not thinking of leaving the theatre, are you?" And of course I said, "Well, I've got to hang up my shoes any moment, and I've got to find a job. This audition came up and I thought, 'That might be fun.'" And he said, "I'm shocked," and about a week later he offered me the chance to be his assistant.

I didn't make any decisions. I never plan. I loved dancing so much I just thought, 'When the day comes I can't dance, I'll think about what else I'm going to do.' I wasn't injured. I saw myself on a video, and I thought, 'The back is beginning to look like an ironing board. I don't think I can go on doing this much longer.' It would have been about '78, '79, and then I started to work with Kenneth, and I didn't go into it convinced I could do it. I said to him, "I've never taken a rehearsal. How do you do it?" and he said, "You jump in the deep end. Next week, I want you to take a corps de ballet rehearsal of *The Four Seasons*, I want to see how you do." I said, "I don't know the first thing about the corps de ballet," and he said, "Then find out."

So I went into the rehearsal and said to the corps de ballet, "I'm telling you that I don't know the first thing about what you do in this ballet. There's no video of it, I don't read notation and I don't know what your first entrance is." They all thought it was ridiculous. I thought it was a very difficult challenge and that somehow Kenneth wanted me to be able to do it. And because he seemed to have the confidence to give me the chance...all I could do was my best. So one of the corps de ballet girls sweetly said, "Our first entrance is the diagonal from upstage," and I said, "And what do you do coming on?" I didn't know it. But I kept trying and of course I got help from some of the girls, and guys too, who said, "No, Kenneth always wants us to emphasize this" or "That pattern's supposed to rotate on the center people..." They helped me.

No, he didn't come, because he knew that would have been... well, pressure. Kenneth was not paralyzing, because he was so quiet. He hardly ever shouted, he never really put people down. If you made him angry, if he thought you weren't trying, if you were changing his choreography without talking to him about why you might want to change it, then he would get furious. But even his fury...He never ranted and raved and stamped his foot and shouted about the place, that wasn't his way, just as Fred never did. They could both say very cutting things, but there weren't tantrums.

Afterwards he said to me, "How did you do?" and I said, "Perhaps you should ask them." I'd witnessed other people who weren't sure. I remember Michael Somes transferring from being a dancer to being at the front of the studio, but he'd also assisted Fred, even when he was still dancing. Michael often asked you, "What's that step really meant to be?" and it never occurred to me that he was asking because he didn't know. I thought he was asking me because I wasn't showing it properly. So there was no role model, and so on I went.

But I went on a triple weekend course run by an American company for people who were concerned about self-esteem, confidence in difficult situations, handling argumentative or aggressive people. It was an amazing experience because it was very confrontational, and what I saw was how many people were unable to handle being confronted. I went to find out if there was a quick sure way to handle fear in front of 40 pairs of eyes, my fear and my uncertainty about how to handle a roomful of people. But of course I was not afraid at all of being confronted, I'd encountered that all through my life as a dancer. The person who was directing the course would come up and stand within a foot of your face and speak at you. He was trying to get me to react, and I was saying to him, "I'm really sorry, I don't know how you're wanting me to respond, but I'm so used to being corrected, to being criticized, that this holds no fears for me." So a tremendous amount of the course for me was spent observing other people's anxieties.

You see, all through my career, I was focused on being a dancer. I'd been married for ten years and I'd divorced my husband, which was, like for anybody, very distressing, frightening, starting out one's life again on one's own, and it was all around the time when I knew I was going to have to stop. But I'm a person who tends to take a day at a time. So each day, as a dancer, I would get up and look forward to going to work and do class and do my rehearsals and think about all my corrections...I was very, very blinkered. I continued to live at home until I was something like 25, until I got married. My father died when I was 13, and I had a stepfather who was always very practical, very caring, a highly intelligent man. And though I'd been so blinkered as a dancer, all the time in my blinkeredness was this figure, who kept saying to me, "What do you think about...? Have you heard about...? I suggest you read this article, just so that we're not talking about ballet at the dinner table again. I'd like to discuss this article over dinner." When we first came to England, he gave me *Three Men in a Boat* and Dodie Smith's *I Captured the Castle* to read, and we used to go to the theatre. He wanted to introduce England to me, and because he'd been in South Africa, he knew the society that I'd come from and he knew the leap that he wanted me to make. He would always say to me, "You're bright and intelligent and I want you to keep your brain working, because you're so fixated about what you're doing—which is fabulous, and we look forward to seeing you on the stage—but you must be as broadminded and have as broad an interest base as you possibly can, because you don't know what's going to happen to you when you stop dancing."

He was relentless in pursuing my brain, but what I didn't have in the rehearsal studio were people skills...well, not enough. To be in the class and then taking [teaching] the class, at least you know the class. But to take a rehearsal when you don't know a step... It's like suddenly being in a room and they're speaking another language. I'd already done quite a bit of teaching of my roles, so I knew I could teach. Kenneth had watched me teaching the mistress [in *Manon*] and three casts of *The Rite of Spring*, and he used to say to me, "I was so impressed by how you did that." That was easy, because I knew it in detail. I adored passing on. I used to want to teach my sister when I was eight and she was four. So I don't think I even thought about how to do it—I just did it, and I guess that's what Kenneth had seen. What was terrifying was...I hadn't been in the corps de ballet for 15 years, I'd left it behind me, and then I was back in, trying to manage a corps de ballet, which of course I had *never* done.

But also, I realized—and I witnessed this on the course—the moment somebody is in an anxious situation, their thought process shuts down and they can't think calmly and clearly. And I realized that when somebody asked me a question and was perhaps testing me in a rehearsal, there must have been a moment of panic, and I knew that I didn't respond as I really wanted to. So the course was a help, and another thing was that I met someone who had been in the police force. I remember saying to him, "How do they go about teaching you to avoid aggressive confrontation?" because the course had not shown me that. And he said, "You mean, like when I have to walk up to a group of six young men who are drunk on a street corner and look as if they're about to throw that brick through the shop window?" I said, "Yes, exactly." He said, "We would play-act it. We played scenes out like that, how you approach them, how slowly you speak, where you put your voice, whether you look at them or you don't. I can do all sorts of exercises with you." That really opened the door for me, and from those exercises...it was wonderful. It makes it sound as if the dancers were very aggressive—they weren't. But of course if dancers feel you're wasting their time or you haven't done your preparation...Kenneth hadn't got them all together and said to them, "Look, I want Monica to…" My name went down on the call sheet, and I turned up, and they thought, 'Mason? What's she doing taking the rehearsal?'

What I found more difficult even than the corps de ballet was rehearsing a principal role that I'd never danced, for instance, *Manon* pas de deux, and not knowing it well enough. When I first found myself rehearsing…it was Wayne Eagling and Marguerite Porter…I'd watched the video a lot, because I'd always seen the ballet from the wings. I'd not really had the chance to go out front and watch, and I hadn't sat at the front of the studio and watched. Also, you have to train your eye…When you're watching the corps de ballet, you're trying to see 16 couples—where do you look? Then just sensibly you think, 'I can't watch those 16 couples. OK, I'll make four, four, four, four do it. Then I'll put eight and eight, and then I'll put 16 together. Fabulous. I'll do that tomorrow.' But when you come to a principal couple, you think, 'Is that on a cou de pied or is that a passé?' Of course I'd have to be honest, I would say, "I don't remember that from the video. I'll go and have another look if you like." So again, little by little you learn how to do it.

But to get meaning across, that for me remains the most fascinating part of any rehearsal. I love trying to get to the bottom of something and help them to resolve it, I love the challenge of saying something 16 different ways and the dilemma when you're not getting through and there's no light going on, and finally someone says, "*That* means something to me. *Now* I understand what you mean." It's very challenging to say something to very senior dancers, correcting Sylvie Guillem, for example, a highly intelligent woman, when she's got a very clear idea of how she wants something to be, and then watching it in a performance and going 'round and saying to her, "I just want to question that moment. What are you trying to convey there?" Of course, she always could explain exactly what she was after and why.

I found it very difficult [when I started coaching] to be correcting the people that I was going to be dancing with the next night. That wasn't easy. But being a dancer isn't easy, and I don't think I ever had thought that anything in life was actually easy, so I wasn't surprised. I think I was very lucky, firstly to have had the audition at the BBC. Because if I hadn't and I hadn't told Kenneth, then what would have happened? Would I have just left, and he would have suddenly looked 'round one day and said, "Where's Mon gone?" But he went and spoke to Norman Morrice [then director of the

Royal Ballet] and said, "I want Monica…" And of course Donald MacLeary had left the company to dance again—he had become ballet master and was assisting Kenneth—so Kenneth really lost his assistant. At that time Kenneth was also involved with ABT [America Ballet Theatre] and starting to transatlantic-hop, so he wanted someone who he knew would be here, looking after his things. I wasn't an assistant to the director—I had nothing to do with Norman. I was Kenneth's assistant.

Then when Norman retired and Anthony [Dowell] took over, I was principal *répétiteur*, and of course I continued to look after the Kenneth ballets. And then I was assistant to Anthony and then I became assistant director. There was a period when I was assisting Kenneth *and* assisting Anthony. That was interesting—I used to feel like the filling in the sandwich. Of course, Anthony and Kenneth always got on, but what I heard on the artistic planning side and what I heard from the principal choreographer meant that I had a huge amount of information and I had to be very discreet and very diplomatic. By then I was feeling much more comfortable about what I was doing…It's *always* a challenge, it never stops being a challenge, and walking into a roomful of people where you've got to be on the ball and deliver for two and a half hours, fully focused, fully concentrating and not missing a trick, is not easy. It doesn't matter how old or young you are, it's a challenge and it's wonderful.

As an assistant I was a negotiator, a diplomat, but of course I had a fabulous job. I was working with some of the finest dancers in the world, I was learning about producing a ballet, planning the rehearsal program, casting it…I used to take my ideas for casting 'round to Kenneth, and we would sit in his kitchen…The first time I attempted a cast list for *Romeo*—it had probably been out of the rep for two or three years—it needed new people going in, and he said to me, "I want you to do it, so that I can see it. Who do you propose for a new Mercutio? Who do you propose for a new Benvolio?" So I'd written them all out, and sitting at his kitchen table he said, "That's an interesting proposal for Mercutio. But that one's very predictable and boring," crossed it out, "not suitable. Why do you think he's suitable for Mercutio?" And I'd say, "Because of this and this." "No, I'll tell you why he's not, because of this and this. You see, what I'm looking for, always, in Mercutio is blah, blah, blah. Go back to the original cast, see what I had in [David] Blair." He never minded casting a small person if a tall person had created a role—heights, sizes, never bothered Kenneth. It was something inside there that he wanted. He said, "Or you can choose somebody really different, and then try and get it out of them. But you can't get out what's not really in. So you need to be sure that you've seen a spark and that you can pull it out somehow."

So I had wonderful times over cups of tea and casting, and a huge education, evaluating every single name on the cast list and discovering yet again how every element is difficult. A cast list is a very difficult thing to get right. You have to think who's done it in the past, how many more times are they likely to do it. If we're going to run 15 shows of *Romeo*, how many casts do I really need? Is there enough time to rehearse five casts? Is that ridiculous? Probably. Cut it down to four. If I'm cutting it down to four, which of those two new people goes in a bracket and which person gets the show? Christopher Newton used to do a lot of cast lists at that time. He was ballet master and he was amazing. He would say, "Your cast list doesn't work at all," and then he'd show me why. There's a system, and he was talking about how to put the names on the paper, how you find an order, how you check you haven't forgotten anybody, and how you have to take the whole company roster and work it against the cast list to make sure you know who's doing this in Act I, who's doing this in Act II. Of course that was an eye-opener; again, I thought, 'This isn't easy either.'

Then, how long do you need for the corps de ballet? How many rehearsals do you want? He used to say, "I always think it's good to start out with, say, an hour and a half. Try to get through these two acts, all the corps de ballet entrances and exits and everything. You haven't got new people to teach? I would give you an hour and a half on Monday. Then I can't give you anything 'til Thursday, and you shouldn't need another hour and a half. Can you manage with an hour? Then on Friday, run it once more in 45 minutes." So everybody feeds you information, everybody helps, and the rest of it you just learn by making mistakes. You come to the end of an hour and you haven't covered everything and everyone's saying, "We've only got 45 minutes tomorrow, and we haven't finished today." And I'll say, "I'm very sorry, that was my error. I thought we'd get through it." It's like everything in life: you only learn by making mistakes. I wanted to be good, as good as I could possibly be at the job I was asked to do. That's all I ever wanted, to be able to do a really good job for the people I was working for. I wanted not to let them down, I wanted to help the dancers. In the end I suppose my ambition was to be the best assistant director anybody could possibly have.

When Anthony left...I didn't apply. Because I didn't see myself as the director. You have to remember, my directors had been Ninette de Valois, Frederick Ashton, Kenneth MacMillan, Norman Morrice, Anthony Dowell, and I didn't see myself in any way capable of doing what they had done. I wasn't a choreographer, I didn't think I could produce a ballet or direct a production. I could only reproduce what I knew Kenneth wanted or whoever was here whose production I was responsible for, that was what I aimed to do, to the absolute best of my capacity. I'm not a competitive person. I never really competed with other dancers. I never saw it like that, which is why I hated dance competitions as a child. I liked running in a race at school and winning, I liked knowing that I could run faster than anybody else, but that was the point of running in a race. But that's not the point of dancing.

And now it's like my directors are all inside me, but of course my experience of them as directors was different according to my station in the company. My experience of de Valois was very little, because she wasn't around a great deal and I was a lowly creature. I can remember doing several soloist things on an American tour when she was the director, coming back to London, and finding that all the solos that I'd danced on the tour were taken away from me and I was back in the corps de ballet. I remember saying to the ballet master, "I've just seen the cast sheet for *The Sleeping Beauty*, and I haven't got a Fairy variation and I haven't got a Florestan and I'm not doing Friends," and he said, "No, dear, I'm very sorry. That's what Madam wants." I thought, 'I wonder what this means. Am I failing completely?' I didn't really dare to ask the question that was most in my mind: Am I about to be sacked because she thinks I'm terrible? I didn't want to know, so I just thought, 'I'll keep going.'

And then later in my life, when I lived in Kew I used to drive her home to Barnes, and we used to have the most amazing conversations. How I didn't crash I'll never know, because she'd ask the most tricky questions and she used to ask my opinion, perhaps of another company visiting London: Had I been to see this company? and What did I think about a repertoire choice they'd made for London? Because, she said, those are the sorts of things you need to think about when you're going to visit a new country, How do you show the company at its best? So *that* went in.

Then there's Fred. There's a huge amount about Fred, because under Fred I became a soloist, and he allowed me to do *Swan Lake*. I asked to have the chance to do this role—I didn't just get it. Deanne Bergsma, Vyvyan Lorrayne and I all went to ask him for one full-length ballet; Vyvyan asked for *Sleeping Beauty* and Deanne and I asked for *Swan Lake*. We didn't share the conversation we had with Fred, except we all came out smiling. We were all given the chance to do our first performances with the touring company and then, if that worked, we would do it in London. I very much remember Fred saying, "Why do you want to do it?" I said, "Because I feel I'm ready to take on a full-length ballet." And he said, "Yes, I would agree with that. What are you going to bring to the role of Odette-Odile to interest me?" So I said I really didn't know, I needed to begin to study the ballet in order to discover how to do it. So he said, "Well, you'll do it in the touring company to start with, and I'll hear how you get on. And then if it's been a success, I probably will try to give you a performance on the next American tour." So I did a matinée in Seattle, and then it was agreed that I should have one here. He said to me after the performance, "You did well, you've got a long way to go with the white act, which I'm sure you know, but I shan't come and see you again." And he never came to another performance.

What is astonishing, looking back, is that I wasn't devastated. I completely accepted the fact that because he was still a major choreographer and his focus was on his ballets, the individual dancers who were *not* his favorites...I was never one of his favorites and I knew that, and that was fine. He didn't stop other people using me, but he didn't choose to use me. So his concentration was on the people that he chose to see. What it meant was that one had to be incredibly self-reliant, incredibly dependent on *other* people, and this is where Winifred Edwards continued to play this extraordinary role. Working with Winifred Edwards was an absolute turning point in my life, because she taught me everything I needed to know about myself as a dancer, about technique, about my technique, and about handling my body. I worked with her every week for ten years, from 20 to 30, the most crucial phase of my career, and she was absolutely instrumental in my development. She would come always to see a leading role that I was dancing—we did pay for our private lessons, but she always bought her own tickets—and then she based her coaching and her further lessons on what she'd seen in your performance. She was a brilliant woman and she would sow little seeds. She would set things in your coaching classes and she would say, "This isn't exactly what you do as Odette, but you'll be able to use this when you go into your rehearsal again." She never wanted to interfere with how we were rehearsed by the company, so she trod this amazing path through the middle.

When Kenneth was director and when he was still making his full-length ballets, we all knew that there was a limit to his energy. He couldn't be out front every night. And when Norman Morrice joined...I remember him asking me what opinions I'd been given of my last act of *Swan Lake*. And I said to him—and he nearly fell over—"I don't think anybody's ever watched my fourth act, not from the front." It was just how life was; you accepted the fact that when Kenneth was preparing *Mayerling* or whatever it was, that was the focus. If you'd been given a leading role in one of those ballets, you weren't about to carp at the fact that two days later, after you'd created the drunken pas de deux [in *Manon*], he wasn't in the audience for your *Swan Lake* performance. It didn't enter my head. Norman watched lots more performances, because he'd decided he wouldn't choreograph while he was the director. Anthony Dowell was not a choreographer, so he attended almost all performances, and I try to do the same.

So that's why I think I've got the incredible practical side of Ninette. I said to her once, "Madam, I know so little. Of course I wasn't around when you first made the Vic-Wells, then the Sadler's Wells Ballet. What was it like to be solely responsible?" She said, "I was never solely responsible. It was always a team, and I always depended on the wonderful people around me. I could never have done it alone. You don't do jobs like that alone." So when I was asked to step in [as director] after Ross [Stretton] left, I put that portrait of her there, looking at me, facing me, knowing that she didn't do it alone, so I must never be alone. I know that the buck stops with me, but I need this incredible team.

That's why I was so keen eventually to have a music director, that's why I really wanted a resident choreographer, because I wanted a policy, and if you don't have a resident person with a real position, you can't ask them to think in terms of long-term. I said to Wayne [McGregor, the Royal Ballet's resident choreographer], "I want you to tell me how *you* see the position. What part does choreography play, not only in this company but in the whole house and with the schools, upper and lower?" When we came to have these wonderful evenings of choreography by the dancers, in a workshop situation in the Clore [Studio] or the Linbury [Theatre, both within the Royal Opera House], I knew that I could say to the dancers, "I thought your piece was really interesting. Did you ever think that you could have made it a little longer?" But I really didn't consider that I was the right person...I could talk to them as a more qualified Joe Public, but I couldn't talk to them about choreography.

If you've never done something...As a student, everybody always wanted me in their piece because I was quick and I was a good team player and I was not embarrassed to do anything. That was always fun, but when I tried to do it I was absolutely useless. The same as trying to write an essay at school—I don't have that kind of creative imagination. So that was one of the reasons I always thought I couldn't be a director, because I didn't feel I had a creative imagination. What I discovered, of course, in being a director, is that you need so many *other* things as well that maybe I could [use] all the things I'd experienced and learnt and struggled with over all those years and maybe somebody wouldn't notice that I didn't write good essays. Except, you see, when we came to do our production of *The Sleeping Beauty*, I discovered that I had all sorts of ideas about how I wanted to do the Transformation scene. I was amazed! I thought, 'Where did I get that idea from? I'm doing the thing I never thought I could do. I don't know what people will think of it, but I'm actually doing it. And I'm doing it because, now I come to think of it, I'm not frightened. I'm just giving free rein to my imagination.'

It is the greatest honor to be director of the Royal Ballet, and it is an enormous responsibility looking after a wonderful roster of talented young people and trying to give as many of them as many opportunities as possible. I started in the Christmas of '02 and the contract was to run until the summer of '05. Then it was extended to '07, and then 'til 2012. If I'd known in '02 that I was going to be here until '12...I'm not saying I think I would have run away. I don't know how I would have reacted. But it was important that I only saw it as a two- or three-year thing to start with, because it was an enormous shock and such an enormous challenge to think that suddenly, my heavens, I'm in the hottest seat.

As long as the people working with the Royal Ballet and directing the rehearsals understand the values that de Valois and Ashton and MacMillan really held most dear, you will keep a quality and a particular kind of fluency and musicality to your dancers. I have no idea of 50 years from now, when the people teaching and running the rehearsals and directing the company never knew those people—the company probably will look very different. I won't be there to see it. You know, one of my favorite moments with Ashton was on tour in America. I can't remember where we were, but there was a pool. It was late afternoon, and I'd come back to the hotel and I remember thinking, 'Perhaps I could just have a little swim. It's so hot.' I went down to the pool and he was sitting there, in a beautiful silk dressing gown, with a drink and his ciggies, and he looked at me and he said, "You're doing Lady Elgar soon, aren't you?" I said, "Yes. I'm really pleased," because I'd waited ages. And he said, "Show me the first step." I was in my bikini, there were other people around the pool, and I was invited suddenly to do that pas de chat step. And immediately, of course, he said, "I knew before you started you wouldn't bend enough." I said, "Well, I'm not in shoes…" He said, "There's no excuse. Your upper body is not expressing the fullness of that movement. You know I want… Touch the grass. Touch the grass!" So when I went on the stage eventually and he came 'round after the show, I said to him, "Did I touch the grass?" and he said, "Yes, you did. But you wouldn't have done if I hadn't told you."

Ashton had an attention to detail that is rare. His insistence in rehearsal on the quality in a movement of the head, the eyeline, exactly how you placed yourself at an angle to somebody else and how you moved away, where you found the light and what you did with it when you'd found it…The incredible detail rubbed off on us, and so we are filled with that information. You try to pass it on to the next generation, and you can see very clearly that nine out of ten people won't get it and then there'll be one. This was something Winifred Edwards used to say to me: "If you go on to teach, you will have dancer after dancer who listens, who does it and then forgets it. Then you'll have somebody who comes in and there's something special. *That's* the link, that will be your next link." And that's what one tries to do. You're trying to find the people that you feel have that extra special understanding of what you're talking about.

The same applies to Kenneth. Kenneth was never as detailed in beautiful things. Fred loved beauty so much; Kenneth loved the physical. That's putting it too simply, but Kenneth let it go a little more wild, more free. Fred had a sort of absolute perfection view, which one was always trying to meet. It wasn't reducing in its demands, but if you suspected that you weren't quite what he saw as his ideal for this particular role, then you might find it inhibiting, because you could fall into the trap of trying to copy someone who you knew had pleased him before. Kenneth always used to say, "Never copy anybody else. I can't bear a copy. I'm rehearsing you and I've chosen you because I want *you*. Now, be you."

When you're young and keen and ambitious, you need to believe that you've got something individual to say yourself. Personally I felt inspired by the people that I'd seen in these ballets. Where I felt daunted was when I attempted *Sleeping Beauty*—I'd watched Margot for years and years being so completely fabulous that I really wondered whether I had something to say that would be interesting to an audience. I'd absorbed her into my memory bank so completely that when it came to the performance, I actually didn't feel I could completely find me, I felt she was lurking in everything I did. Whereas I didn't feel that in *Swan Lake*, because the ballet suited me much better, the dramatic aspect allowed me to find something much more personal to say.

Remember that today they watch an awful lot of DVDs—we didn't have that—and it informs them in some way. Of course it's not like seeing a live show, but it does allow them to study many, many interpretations of these roles, and then to perhaps see which of those interpretations they are most sympathetic to. But there is a huge danger of imitation, and I think imitation is horrible. Inspiration is quite a different thing and discernment is quite another thing and finding your own voice.

The company today...Madam made the Australian ballet, she made a Canadian national ballet, she made a Turkish ballet, we traveled the length and breadth of America...What I see is how the ballet exploded: Madam, Fred, Rudolf [Nureyev], Margot, Margot-and-Rudolf. Classical ballet had an absolute rebirth in the '60s and '70s, an explosion across the States, even in Europe, building audiences everywhere. And inevitably, people in Australia wanted to dance in Australia. South Africans wanted to dance in South Africa, Canadians want to live and dance where they were born. They don't all want to come to England. Whereas once upon a time, you *had* to come here, there was only one place to come. I couldn't go to Moscow. I could have gone to New York and done an audition for Balanchine, but my mother brought me to London. This was the honey pot, so all the bees flew in to this honey pot. But as the companies grew around the world, then of course you had a need for more choreographers. But how can you grow Balanchines, MacMillans and Ashtons? You can't. So now we're in this predicament where there are all these companies and not enough rep to go around. There is not enough repertoire in the world. There are not enough choreographers. And there are certainly not enough choreographers making full-length ballets. What do you do? You start to borrow. It's like suddenly there aren't enough clothes, so you've got to borrow your clothes from all over the place, and then you're wearing a Russian sweater with an American T-shirt and Spanish shoes and a French hat.

For the Royal Ballet...It would seem to me that when Ashton brought [Bronislava] Nijinska here he was thinking, 'This is the woman I most admired as a choreographer, and these are the ballets that will suit this company. We must get *Les Biches* and *Les Noces* on the stage at the Royal Opera House.' When Kenneth brought Jerry Robbins and Glen Tetley, he wanted their ballets for this company, on this big stage. You're trying to get the people that can work with a big company in a major opera house. That's why now, when I'm looking at all kinds of different choreographers, the questions in the front of my mind are, Could this person really do something for the Royal Ballet? How are they going to develop the history of the Royal Ballet? *Are* they going to, or...Why am I interested in this person?

When I'm looking at workshops and the Linbury, I've got a different context, because I'm thinking, 'I want to bring this person because I saw [his work] somewhere else and I really liked how he used the dancers.' But to put that person on the main stage immediately? No, I wouldn't do that. I'd try them out first somewhere else. Another choreographer might be the flavor of the month, and I go and see a work and I think, 'That's a marvelous piece, but it's not going to work for us, because our dancers are not like those dancers. Is that person capable of adapting what they do to bring out something special from the dancers we have?' When de Valois brought [Leonide] Massine, she knew, because of the way she'd trained her dancers, that Massine could work with those dancers. Fred knew Nijinska could work with us, Kenneth knew Tetley and Robbins could work here.

You're thinking of people's progress, but at the same time, I believe the repertoire comes first. I've always said that the choreographers are the kings and the dancers serve the choreographers.

The dancers in this company know that, and that's why they're never cavalier with choreography. You don't just change choreography because you feel like it. You serve that work, just as a musician serves a score. You don't play Mozart how you feel like playing Mozart. You don't change Shakespeare. The text is the text, and that is what you serve. The classics are our heritage, and each generation of classical dancers wants to measure themselves in the classics. Of course they've evolved over the years. What one's trying to do with something like MacMillan is be as loyal to the choreographer's original intention as you possibly can. You don't want to change the steps. With the classics, the steps have inevitably changed anyway, long before you did it, and so...I obviously don't feel the same loyalty to Petipa that I do to MacMillan, because I don't know really what Petipa originally did.

As a dancer, I always used to say to myself, What is the intention? Why these steps? because the steps express something. If you're doing a ballet where you're in a black leotard and pink tights, not in a costume that displays you as something, and your best friend is the music, what is the intention when each step meets each bar of music? I could never learn anything in an abstract way, not when you're thinking of the performance. The moment you've got a grasp of the shape of something, you then look for what you're going to invest in this shape to communicate something. Because the moment you've got to say something, you have to have something in your head to say.

I suppose I'm always trying to find the next piece of new work, of course we want new work, but what's become harder is that we're doing 135 shows a year and we used only to do about 100, so you cannot be doing the same numbers of new ballets. Dancers can only work six hours a day, and 35 shows is 35 times three hours of performing, which is 35 times three hours when you can't be making a new ballet or rehearsing. So those three hours are crucial, and all of that has to be computed in when you're looking at a new work. I can't ask somebody to come here to make a new ballet and then...If they say to me, "I'm going to need between 80 and 100 hours in the rehearsal studio," and we say, "Actually, all we can give you is 65 to 70 max," they're going to say, "Well, I can't do it."

I definitely wouldn't do more performances. We did 145, I think, in '05–'06, and we nearly died. And that's 145 *here*, not including the tour; we do about 160 all in. That's the decision of the house. Performances make money, should make money, so…And the dancers get used to it. You've also got people who like doing lots of performances, and of course you really develop dancers in performance, not in rehearsal. I think they are better looked after now than they were in the past because we know more about how to look after them. We know how to train them and how not to overtrain them, we know how to take care of them with the physiotherapy and the Pilates and the massage. You tread a very fine line, but all the time one's trying to push the boundaries without killing people…ideally. When I say to most directors that we do 135 shows and 12 programs, they faint at the number. "How do you do 12 programs? You're only performing for ten months of the year." I say, "We change programs every three weeks." "How do you do that?" "By working flat out six days a week."

We have to change that often, because we cannot run a triple bill for ten shows—it absolutely doesn't sell. We know that it sells for about six or seven; to maximize a triple bill, six or seven is it. That's why we push our luck with the things that we know do sell, like the full-length ballets. When someone writes a review and says, "It feels like yesterday we saw *Romeo and Juliet*," it wasn't yesterday. We never do the same full-lengths two years running. You need people to help you with triple bills, I need critics to write about them in a way that's going to make people want to come. You do everything you can to educate them. You do insight evenings, you do as much press as you can possibly afford. And actually the audience are much better about triples than they used to be when they were the same price as full-lengths. Triple bills have sold much better since they cost less than full-lengths.

The Diaghilev ballets [we're reviving] are wonderful works, and there are always people who haven't seen them and always dancers who haven't danced them. Your life as a dancer is enriched by dancing wonderful works, which is why I can't possibly do new work just for the sake of doing new work, not when there are those treasures in the cupboard. For *Firebird*, the link is that Karsavina taught Margot, and Margot was rehearsed by [Lubov] Tchernicheva and Serge Grigoriev. When I came to learn *Firebird*, Ann Jenner and I had an amazing hour with Margot, that one rehearsal was packed with information, and we both afterwards scribbled notes to remind each other of all the things she'd said. So when I then came to teach Leanne Benjamin and Mara Galeazzi, I was saying, "Margot said

Karsavina said that Fokine said…" So if either of those girls were to teach it at some point, they will say, "I learned this from Monica Mason, who learned it from Margot, who was taught by…" and on we go.

We don't do Massine ballets anymore in the Royal Ballet, we haven't done a Massine ballet in years. So, they get lost. They just fade away. The last time we did *Les Biches*, which is very much *not* about just learning steps…Each time you do *Les Biches*, you've got a generation that's further and further away from the period, and it doesn't matter how much you talk to them and how many photographs you pin on the board and how much information you print out so that they can read it in the dressing room. Then you maybe only do five performances. You can't really get to grips with it, so I feel it becomes harder and harder to do justice to those ballets. And if you know that you might have to get it on in a particularly busy rehearsal period, sometimes you wouldn't do that ballet because you wouldn't have sufficient time to really convey everything about it to those dancers in order that they could really grasp the underlying history and the meaning and the quality and the sensibility of it.

Again, that's the balancing act. Is there enough time to get *Les Biches* on properly, given the fact that in that triple bill I want to do a new work? Do I not do a new work? Do I do two "bring-backs" of a recent new work, one of which is *Biches*, or do I do a new ballet? Those are the decisions that one struggles with, and eventually you have to make a decision. Is it better to do *Les Biches* with a little less rehearsal time than you would like? Or even maybe thinking, 'Have I got an ideal Hostess at the moment?' of course remembering that you're making that decision for four years hence. I have no idea who will even be here three or four years from now. Who will the three men be in *Biches*? I have no idea. Of course in the planning you don't have to have absolutely everything watertight four years in advance, thank heavens. You leave a TBA, which is "To be announced," you leave TBAs sometimes all over the place, or you also say a bring-back without knowing what that's going to be.

There has to be new work every season, brand-new work. How much you can manage to do depends to an extent on how the schedule pans out. Somebody has to start with a plan. Because the opera are always planned even further ahead than we are and because we work so easily and well together, the opera start, and they lay their operas out. The person who does this knows the sort of spread the ballet requires in terms of how many shows a week and sharing out Mondays and Saturdays so we don't end up with a program where the ballet are on every single Monday or every single Saturday for six weeks. Scheduling is probably the most complex thing that we do, because...I'm struggling to explain it...No two months are the same and no two seasons are the same, and so everything is created anew every single season. Which is why sometimes we have a month where we might have 25 performances and another month we might have 15. That also dictates where the new work could come, because obviously, if you're trying to get a new work done and you've got 25 shows in that month, that slot is usually better as a bring-back. But a month that has 18 shows in it or maybe less is a very good month to lead up to a new ballet, because we'll have rehearsal time. Because, I said it before, every performance is three hours' lost rehearsal time. That's for corps de ballet. The principals can work six hours a day *and* perform, but you wouldn't do that to principals because you wouldn't have them working 'til half-past five and performing that evening.

I want very much to explore whatever talent I can find within the company, because we have a tradition of doing that. There was always a very strong experimental choreographic aspect to the Royal Ballet, going way back; it was a policy of the company that this should happen. Peter Wright and Kenneth MacMillan have talked about working with John Cranko in this little theatre in Henley-on-Thames, and by the time I joined the company in the mid-'50s we were doing...I think it was called Sunday Ballet Club...whenever a theatre could be found. For Leslie Edwards, who ran the Choreographic Group for 20 years, '60s to the '80s, the biggest problem was finding a venue, and now we have facilities in the house. Leslie was always fighting to find these young people enough time; to start with he might have ten or twelve people, and by the time we got to the [performance] we had five or six, because the others hadn't had enough time [to rehearse]. Here, when we do something in the Clore or the Linbury, those evenings are prepared in the company time. Plus the fact that all those years when we were at Baron's Court, we had to be out of the building by 6:30, the caretaker had to lock up, whereas here, people can work 'til 10:00 at night, you could work on longer if you wanted. You can always get out of the building. And there are five studios to play with, so it's a completely different ballgame.

Today's choreographers appear, to my body memory, to be making more demands physically. But of course, over the 30 years, bodies have become more accustomed to different demands. If we were to do *Les Biches* now, all those repeated entrechats quatre are an incredible challenge to a young dancer, because Nijinska always said, "You don't need to plié to jump. You just jump." So she set all this incredible *terre à terre* work, where you really used the strength in your feet to jump. Now, that doesn't *appear* as physically demanding as Billy Forsythe or Wayne McGregor, but I can assure you it is *just* as demanding. And it would be just as demanding to a young dancer today, because they don't do so much *batterie* anymore. If you'd grown up with Fred and Massine and then you had Nijinska, it was a sort of natural flow. Now they're getting used to Billy Forsythe and Wayne McGregor, and there's a pattern to that.

But then to do Bournonville or Fairy variations…It's very difficult. They have to prepare their bodies and their minds in a different way. It takes…well, not longer than it took us, it just takes a certain amount of time, and you have to build that into your schedule. You have to allow for the fact that every ballet requires something different. Even if you're dancing *Swan Lake* and *Sleeping Beauty* and Fred's *Cinderella* alongside one another, they're different. *Beauty* and *Lac* are closer, *Cinderella* has all sorts of monstrously difficult fast footwork and a different way of moving. For the season coming up, we've got Mats Ek's *Carmen* being rehearsed alongside *Bayadère*. Now, that's really tough, and there was no other way to make it work. We sat for hours to try to reschedule that, and I couldn't do it. So rather than not do *Carmen*, we put it in. Then you try to cast the performances to help the dancers who've got to deal with that very difficult physical demand.

I'm always greedy about having as much work as possible in the company. I probably err on the side of too much work. The marketing policy in the opera house discourages us from repeats, like a part of a triple bill coming back the following season with two new elements and then two of those elements coming back later in that season with one new element, which is exactly how programs used to run when I was a young dancer. We're discouraged from doing that because there is some evidence that they sell less well than a brand-new triple bill. I look back over what I've done since I've been director, and I wonder if I've stretched everybody hugely in some of the seasons, because to have three new pieces in a bill has really pushed everyone, dancers and staff. But the question I ask myself all the time is, Would I buy a ticket for this bill? Would I want to come and see it? That's how I measure it, really.

For anybody who is of a curious mind…I was a child that used to drive people mad with my questions and I still ask lots of questions, and it interests me when I look at young dancers and wonder why they don't appear to be curious enough…and also, when you see somebody who asks a question and then doesn't really listen to the answer. Or someone who has access to an inspirational person and doesn't tap into it at all. There's that wonderful thing of "When the pupil's ready, the teacher's there," and so many people seem to me to be unready, so that even when they're facing someone who could really help them, they don't make use of it or recognize it. When I look back over my life, I think the opportunity to be inspired is what I've loved most of all.

Art matters in our lives hugely. The opportunity for imagination and inspiration and creativity and the freedom to think is what cultivates us and separates us from primitive creatures. The world is full, full, full of information, and we've only got a tiny grain of sand of it. I think, 'When I'm retired, am I going to come back and teach? Am I going to go somewhere else and teach? Or am I going to go off and do something completely different? Am I going to study, and learn about botany, or…?' I don't know. There are millions of things out there, and if one had the great good fortune to go on for the rest of one's life learning about great people…My life has been so extraordinarily fortunate, for it to have been touched by so many great people. I could never have foreseen any of that when I was a child growing up in Johannesburg. How did it happen? It's been the most privileged, blessed and wonderful life.

Thirty years from now, heaven knows where we'll be. Even somebody as great as Diaghilev…In that 20 years, the astonishing things he achieved. But my god, he struggled. He was struggling every week to pay their salaries and struggling for the money for the next score and the next design. He couldn't plan for the future, and I think that de Valois wanted to be a step ahead of that. She wanted to be in a position where the company had more security and eventually a pension plan and a benevolent fund and some medical insurance, something to give dancers some sort of security for their brief careers. But even she, I'm sure, couldn't see where it would be in 30 years. She used to tell Anthony Dowell,

"The situations that you deal with daily now are very different from the ones I dealt with, and I think sometimes maintaining something is harder than growing it in the initial stages. We didn't know really what the future would be. But now you're having to maintain it, and life is so much more complex now than it was."

My own future...I don't know. Having always had one's life completely planned by other people and having never really made a decision, when I wake up one day and think, 'My goodness, I haven't got a call sheet, I haven't got to be anywhere at a certain time,' I wonder whether I'll completely fall apart at the seams.

London
November 2008

Desmond Kelly

Desmond Kelly (b. Penhalonga, Southern Rhodesia (now Zimbabwe), 1942) began his ballet training at the age of nine with Elaine Archibald. He came to London in 1957 on a Royal Academy of Dancing scholarship and studied with Ruth French before entering London Festival Ballet (1959–1965) and acquiring soloist and principal roles in ballets ranging from *Les Sylphides* and *Napoli* to *Bourrée Fantasque* and *Etudes*. Between 1965 and 1970 he performed with the Zurich Opera Ballet, the National Ballet in Washington, D.C. and the New Zealand Ballet, where he was also ballet master and, briefly, the company's director. When he joined the Royal Ballet as a principal in 1970, he added contemporary works by Ashton, MacMillan, Cranko and Balanchine to his classical repertory, also creating roles in Tetley's *Field Figures* (1970) and *Laborintus* (1972). After six years, he transferred to Sadler's Wells Royal Ballet (which became Birmingham Royal Ballet in 1990), where he continued to dance classical roles until 1984 and character parts until his retirement in 2008.

§§§

As if performing was not challenging enough, Kelly became ballet master of Sadler's Wells Royal Ballet in 1978, assistant to the director in 1988 and assistant director in 1990. He had a particular responsibility for the Balanchine works in the repertory, and traveled internationally to teach and stage the nineteenth- and twentieth-century classics that he also oversaw at home. In 2006, he led the company's educational collaboration with the charity Youth at Risk to create a television series, *Ballet Changed My Life – Ballet Hoo!*, documenting 18 months of preparation for a stage performance of MacMillan's *Romeo and Juliet*.

Having retired from BRB in July 2008, in September of that year he began a four-year stint as the artistic director of the Elmhurst School for Dance in Birmingham. Two months later, he set aside his non-existent lunch hour to talk to me in his office, often interrupting himself to respond to the needs of his staff and students. I only understood how thoroughly his world had changed when I heard him addressed as Mr. Kelly, probably for the first time in his life.

§§§

At the very beginning, the hook was physicality and getting the muscular satisfaction. I could run faster than the other boys, and I knew I was going to be much better at the high jump, I *was* much better at the high jump, because of what I was doing in my dance classes. We can't bring art into this yet, because I was only about ten years old.

We're not talking about a sudden bolt of revelation from heaven—I'm talking about why I got into it in the first place. And then…I can only say it's like a ladder, one rung at a time. That's discovery, that's interest, that's looking ahead to the next rung, saying, "Oh, I want to know about that." The last rung is this rung, because once I moved into the educational aspect of dance and when I realized how much dance education can do for a human being, then I knew I had done all that stuff before so I could become a teacher. But I didn't know that when I was doing all that stuff, I had no idea. I had the best time in the world, I yummed everything I did in dance, physically, artistically, mentally. What it does for you when you dance, it's incredible, and that was my life. But it was like a revelation when I moved into education, and all of that was preparation.

I could choose so many influences, all the way through my career. Anton Dolin was the first one, whom I ended up by hating because he was a sheer and utter bastard, but he was inspirational in a way. I mean, he gave me opportunities early and recognized…my potential, I suppose, and gave me encouragement and kept me going onto the next stage. Because when you first come from a place like Africa and you've been nine months in a private ballet school [in England] and then you join an international company like London's Festival

Ballet, can you imagine the transition that I had to make? I was 16 years old, having never been away from Africa in my life. So he was the first kind of guide that led me through.

After that, the teacher Andrew Hardie; my wife [Denise le Comte], a very important person in my life for inspiration and sorting my mind out for me; and Peter Wright [former director of Sadler's Wells Royal Ballet] was the latest one, of course. I said to him later, "I was so pleased that you gave me the opportunity to be ballet master," and he said, "You *asked* to be ballet master," and apparently I did. He said, "Why do you want...?" and I said, "I'm interested in rehearsing and teaching the company." He gave me my first break; it wasn't as ballet master, it was as *répétiteur*. And by that stage, dancing was too painful. Late '70s, so how old was I? Was I 40? You do a four-act ballet and you don't recover for three days afterwards. When did I stop dancing? As opposed to pointing my suit in the right direction? Oh god, I don't know. The last thing I did was the Merchant in David Bintley's *Beauty and the Beast*.

So the progression was *répétiteur*, assistant ballet master, ballet master, and I took to it like a duck to water—I just *love* telling people what to do, isn't it awful. But it takes belief in oneself. You can't tell somebody else to do something which you don't believe in yourself. If I'm putting on *Romeo and Juliet* or *Swan Lake* or anything, I have to believe it's the best thing in the whole wide world.

Going back to Andrew Hardie...I used to write his classes down if they interested me on that particular day, and I still have the book with his classes. After I joined the company, Denise and I used to go...in those days you went to outside classes and you paid for them. I was 18, 19, and I didn't know that I was going to teach later but I used his classes when I first started to teach—that was in New Zealand. When you and I talked in '79, I was *répétiteur* or something like that [for Sadler's Wells Royal Ballet], but I planned to teach, absolutely. For god's sake, teaching is the most incredible thing. To see an improvement in somebody in front of your very eyes over a period of time is the most life-enhancing experience you could possibly imagine. Of course you go into it with trepidation, you're bloody nervous. But then personality, musicality, brain power, all that stuff combines, and if your class is a success and your feedback is successful, then that encourages you to go on to the next thing. So things progress.

I'm *still* not qualified. I've been teaching for 25 years and I'm still not qualified, because I don't have anything [official] written down on paper. There's a new government scheme coming into teaching in this country: you have to have certain, specific qualifications to teach in any school. It's going to be…rubbish, it's rubbish, an arbitrary setup of just ticking boxes by probably nobody with a dance background. It means that almost my entire staff are not qualified to teach although they have been professional dancers and their collective knowledge is mind-boggling. How can I say to these people, "You're not qualified, you have to leave"? It's absolutely ridiculous.

I suppose at first you teach yourself. That's why people say when you become a teacher, you learn more than you did when you were a pupil. You actually improve, even from a technical point of view. When you have to understand what you're teaching and articulate that, it goes into your own body and brain. I was teaching and dancing at the same time, but it wasn't 'til later, that, wow, I realized it's because I was teaching that I was getting better.

I taught a lot of summer schools, I taught Cecchetti, I taught RAD [the Royal Academy of Dancing syllabus]. Although I don't know anything about Cecchetti I still taught in the Cecchetti summer schools in Canada and America—it's extraordinary. They wrote to me and said, "Please come and teach," so I went. I didn't teach Cecchetti style, but I did three or four open classes a day, and I suppose…It's so strange, your mind goes back without even realizing it. I had an RAD background, I did open classes and I did lots of Cecchetti classes when I first joined Festival Ballet, so when you go and teach a "Cecchetti" summer school, of course some of it comes out. My style of teaching is an amalgamation of all the teachers I've had, plus ideas of my own, and I teach everyone in the same way. The only adaption I've had to make is between men and women and age groups. That's the only thing. I have to try and impart my knowledge or what I think of dancing to that person. If they're receptive they take it; if they're not, they don't.

What's hardest to instill in dancers? Everything's hard. For me it starts with the musicality—that's the most important thing, the first thing. You can't dance without being musical. You have to understand the music, and it's the music that makes you dance—that's why we dance *to* music. Then the physicality and muscularity after that and the understanding of the steps, which is quite different to the understanding of the role. Take Siegfried in *Swan Lake*. You could perceive this person as being a complete nutcase who falls in love with a swan and has no personality, because a lot of the choreography in *Swan Lake* doesn't lend itself to expression of a character. So the dancer does research, and also in conversation with me or whoever's coaching, finds a way of making a character out of this person.

Making a character out of a classical prince is one of the hardest things possible. It's easy to do things like *Prodigal Son*, when you've got something to grab onto, it's there for you to take. But with princes, cardboard cutouts...Unfortunately, they're still danced like that sometimes today, based entirely on how many pirouettes and double tours a person can do during the course of the evening. Now, understanding the steps...well, it's teaching muscle memory for the steps and the joining of those steps to the character, they can't be separate. The steps are because of the character, not in addition to or a sideline of. If you're doing the first-act variation in *Swan Lake*, the lament variation, you express an emotion, right? You express loneliness, melancholy, 'What am I going to do with my life?', all those things come out in the steps, and you teach that at the same time as you're teaching the role.

Let's just say about *Prodigal Son*—I can get *really* fired up about *Prodigal Son*, and that's important. I have to tell that person how excited *I* was and that I hope they're going to be the same way. Because I danced so many of Mr. B's ballets, and quite a few of Kenneth's, I have been *in* there, dancing those roles to the very best of my ability, with a lot of help from Kenneth [MacMillan] and from Mr. B [Balanchine]. Now I'm out here watching somebody else do the role, so I have to imagine myself still in there and repeat and pass on to that person from the outside what I was given and the experiences I had doing that role and also enthusiasm and energy and belief. All those things are important when you're teaching.

Ballets are written down. You learn ballets. You teach the ballet as written down. It's not enough. We're only 25 percent there. You know the role, you know the choreography—now let's start learning it, because you have to present what you've learned to the public. They're paying the money, you have to make them interested and entertained. So that's where it starts. For a lot of dancers, that's where it ends: 'I've learned the choreography, I can do double tours and ten pirouettes, I know this ballet.' It's not the end, it's a beginning.

The young people's approach to dance is completely different now. You start with hierarchy. When I joined Festival Ballet, if a principal walked down the corridor I would back away to the wall. OK, that's an extreme case. Now, in 2008, that does not exist anymore in schools or in companies, a respect for the hierarchy of the company and the desire, because of the respect, to emulate that person. Now a lot of it is based on 'I'm a better dancer than him, even though he's a principal and I'm not, because I can do ten pirouettes and he can only do four.' It's very, very step-based, very technical. I'm not deriding it, it's a really good thing, but it becomes single-minded. There's so much more to our art form.

Dance is a full-time job...without being a bunhead. You know what a bunhead is? It's someone who, 24 hours, eats, sleeps, talks dance. You have to have a balance, but how can you learn all we have to learn about dance if you're doing other interesting and important things at the same time? I have to be careful here, because I was about to say how important it is to read, to go to the movies, to see drama, to go to art galleries. I'm saying it to the kids here all the time, and they're like this, tunnel vision, on ballet. I hope eventually my saying it will make a difference and I can actually prove to them that becoming a rounded person enhances what you do in dance. It *has* to. At BRB, a lot of them are interested in art, but not the younger generation—they don't even read a book. In fact there was one boy that was having problems emotionally, with girl friends and injuries and all that stuff, and I said, "You've got to occupy...Read. Read interesting books." And he said, "I *hate* reading. I've only ever read one book in my entire life."

It's different too because they're motivated much more by material gain now than we were. You only have to look at the clauses that are forced into contracts, new clauses every year, to know that they expect a good remuneration for what they do now, which was not in our minds when we were young. We didn't expect anything because there wasn't anything. Companies were very, very poor, and...I can't say it was a privilege to dance, but we were very thankful to get what we got. Somebody left BRB a couple of years ago, disgruntled, they went into the outside world, and then came back and said, "You guys don't know how lucky you are, and you keep fighting for more and more." Money! It's money. Because in the bad world out there, he was earning half of what he was earning in the ballet company, not looked after, no medical, insurance, pension scheme, all the perks they get in companies these days. Which is great, this is the way we should go forward, but they shouldn't pay so much attention to material gain.

Absolutely it was part of my job [at BRB] to motivate. If you'd said "inspire," I would have gone for that more, because when I was young, I did need inspiration. Rudolf [Nureyev], Margot [Fonteyn], everyone had inspiration from other people, and I hope I was able to give it in some degree to the dancers I really cared about who I knew cared about dance.

As assistant director...Peter said to me, "You have been assistant *to* the directors and now I'd like you to be assistant director, so that I feel I can go away, leave the company in your hands, and things will continue as was without me worrying about it." Which is exactly what happened. It's *not* a job—it's a title for doing anything and everything. It's a job that you make up yourself. Darcey Bussell once said, "Assistant directors do nothing," and I've often meant to take her to task. Assistant directors are *not* people that do nothing in the background. I did everything. It started with paperwork: I did casting, I worked out how many people are in ballets, how many rehearsals we needed per ballet and who was going to be in them. Then I taught and then I taught ballets and then I rehearsed them, then I put ballets on the stage. I started to make the job for myself, and when I was asked to make a list of job responsibilities it went on for pages. But it's because I'm like that, I like to be busy, I like to have influence wherever I possibly can. And really, I'm not a very nice person, pushing myself around all over the place, shouting at people, telling them what to do.

But I was able, I hope, because I'd reached a certain age and some maturity, to give advice on all sorts of levels, personal as well as professional. I could have one-to-ones with people and draw them out. That was a very important part of my job, to make contact on a personal level with the dancers. They need it. A lot. All dancers need it. Dancers are very insecure people, you must have found that out. As they began to realize that my door was never closed and that I was really interested in every single one of them—with a few exceptions, there are always exceptions—they learned that they could come and they could trust what I said to them.

They're expected to do much more difficult steps now, the technical requirement is much higher in the new works than it was when we were young. So I demand much, much more from them in class than like ten years ago, especially the men, because I know what they have to face in the choreography. You have to prepare them. In fact, we take a specific step...In *Nutcracker* the Ivans do what we call "cobblers," a very low crouch with kicks, which is very hard on the knees. Our approach to that is to prepare them with exercises for two weeks before they even do the first cobbler.

That's where the relation to dance injuries comes in. I think the mind set, the approach to injury, has definitely changed. We were more 'I've got to get back on, I'll take care of it.' Now it's much more what I call mollycoddling. We have a center, its title is blah blah [the Jerwood Centre] for the Prevention of Dance Injuries. I would like to rename it blah blah for the Encouragement of Dance Injuries, because it does, in a way, encourage dancers to rely on being made better for a niggle very quickly, surrounded by equipment and experts, whereas when we were young, we just jolly well had to get on with it. When I first joined the Royal Ballet, it was a revelation—there was a physiotherapist! One physiotherapist. My god, let's all get excited. So that's a huge change, and it's debatable whether to give so much obvious help—'It's there for me if I want it'—whether that does actually encourage the mind to say, 'I am injured, I need help.' Maybe I'm being unfair but I don't think I am.

The audience hasn't changed at all. It's such a disappointment. It's still middle-class, middle-aged women who, as far as I can see, make up the majority of audiences of every dance performance I go to. Why, I don't know. David Bintley [director of BRB] has made *enormous* efforts to get young people involved and he has had some success, but not the dramatic turnaround that I would like and expect. There are not enough young people coming to classical dance as audiences, and I think probably the opposite in contemporary dance. Young people are much more interested, certainly in the London area, in seeing contemporary dance. Classical dance can be perceived as being very old-fashioned, very stiff, and unrepresentative of what's going on in the world these days. You can point to all of those things, but at the core, the heart of classical ballet, is an enormous celebration of art and what art can do for a person's psyche and personality. It's that core which has always fascinated me, and I still would much rather watch *Swan Lake* than watch a contemporary piece. I went to Australia last year to do *Nutcracker* for Peter [Wright] with the Australian company, and after having put it all on here [for BRB], I discovered *more*. Every time I have anything to do with *Nutcracker*, I find another nuance that I hadn't realized before.

Go out there into the corridor and ask any child that goes past what they want to do when they leave the school. They want to dance *Swan Lake*, *Giselle*, *Nutcracker*, the classics. It's what they all aspire to. I got an enormous amount of satisfaction out of dancing these roles, and I think what I got from classical ballet made me into the person I am now, a much more rounded individual. When I came into this job, I asked, "Why do you want me?" and the answer was, "Because you're such a rounded person." I thought that was such a great answer, and I can lay that at the door of classical dance.

We weren't encouraged to delve into the history of our art form, although in later life I did research on my roles—if you're doing *Romeo and Juliet*, of course you read the play. But my swotting up only went as far as that. I was never interested in "the history" of dance, but I think it's becoming increasingly important, and they're taught it now in this school. We have one boy who joined BRB from Elmhurst, his *passion* is history of dance, and he knows much more than I ever knew about it. So there's that kind of personality, and I could show you another student who would say, "No, I don't want anything to do with that. It's rubbish. I'm only interested in what we're doing now."

But tradition is an inspiration, definitely. If you got rid of this strata of teachers, choreographers, *répétiteurs*, people who've done the roles and who are teaching [them] now, from Monica Mason through David Bintley through me through all these thousands of people...If you take that away, what happens to these young people coming up? What have they got to look up to, be taught by? I'm not just talking about technique. I'm talking about "I've done this role, and I can actually show you things that I found out about the role that were never taught." Take those people away, what's left? Nothing. And I think if you sat the dancers here with a tape recorder and made them answer the question [about tradition], they would admit that it's vital.

I can take myself back to doing *Peer Gynt* [by Vaslav Orlikowsky], first three-act ballet I'd ever done in my life, 19 years old. Not coached; taught steps. I was taught the steps and left to find out about the character myself, because in those days the ballet master probably didn't have time or interest. Now today, these kids get...David Bintley choreographs, right? He tells them the story, what he aims for, the music, the background. We just went into rehearsal and they said, "All right, do this step and do that step." That doesn't happen anymore. From David down, through the ballet masters and ballet mistresses, one-to-one coaching is always available for the kids, always. It's still breakneck speed... more breakneck at my end, years ago. We did more ballets in a shorter time and never had enough rehearsal time. Now they don't have enough rehearsal time, but they have more rehearsal time than we had, and they do probably more full-lengths, less one-acts.

The public don't like ballet—you know that. They see the word "ballet" and immediately switch off—we're talking about a majority of people in this country. That's why I'm interested in dance education, not just for the kids but for spreading the word. I've got a PVP program here, a pre-vocational program, which Mary [Goodhew, former director of Elmhurst] started about three years ago. They come in every Saturday, they're eight, nine and ten years old and they have never been exposed to dance before. They do a ballet class, a character class, jazz class, a contemporary class and they have a ball. It's just fantastic—every studio, *packed* with these kids. They pay six pounds for the whole day at the moment, and I want to cut that completely. The parents come as well. They're not allowed to watch, but I'm changing all that, and I'm making a PVP parents association.

That's how we start. I want kids off the street, I want kids that don't have any money...they have talent and no money, I want them in the school and I want them to get interested right from the beginning. I want to go back further than the education program and the schools program at BRB. I want to go back to Year Three, that's like seven years old. Get them interested.

Ballet Hoo! was Will Tuckett's idea, bless him. He took it to a TV company and said, "Let's get some people off the street and teach them how to dance. And let's put them into a production and let's film it." That's how it started. Several companies, mentioning no names, were asked if they'd take on the project—all refused. Came to BRB, presented the project, and David Bintley said, "Yes, please."

Then the project started to change slightly. They thought, 'Let's bring in a social aspect to it. Let's go for underprivileged [young people]. Let's do a ballet that reflects their lives. Let's put them on stage, with full orchestra. Can we do it?' David Bintley said, "Yes, we can. Desmond, I want you to take over." I was so excited about the whole thing, and David could see it, he could read me like a book.

It was a personal challenge, because I said right from the beginning, "If through this project we can get one of those young people off the street, off drugs, off drink, off smoking, off using knives, off the things that they were doing, get one person who'll see a door open and this incredible world out there—Art! Ballet! Music! Theatre!...If they can just see it, I'll be happy. One." How many? On the stage we had 60, and at least ten came out with that.

I needed a combination of things, starting with authority, but then...These damaged children came in with no self-belief, having been told their entire lives that they're rubbish at everything they've done. So you bring authority into that and straightaway they'd say to themselves, 'This is a repetition exactly of what we've been going through our whole lives.' So it was authority used with discretion, making them believe in themselves, which I've been doing my whole life, starting with me, trying to make me believe in myself and then our dancers the same thing. So that was easy, and...I hoped that they would have respect for me because I showed I had respect for them, and that was the result.

I tried not to think about success. It was such an enormous thing to do that in the beginning I didn't know what to do with them. I thought, 'I'll just put them in the background.' Then I saw their enthusiasm and actually the degree of talent with many of them, so I brought them forward a little bit. Then I thought, 'Why not give them some of the bloody major roles, the non-dancing roles?' So we cast them, Marion [Tait, ballet mistress of BRB] and myself. Then it came to the question of Tybalt, and this extraordinary young man...We were only allowed to mention first names in the project, so his first name's Linden. I wanted him to do Act I, and then a professional dancer would take over for the other two acts. He was so good in Act I, he said, "Oh, please, could I not do Act II as well?" I said, "No, you can't. The fights are too complex. I can't risk my Romeos being hurt if you don't know the choreography of the fighting." He said, "Do you have a video?" So I gave him the video. He came back after the weekend, he knew every single move. I said, "I don't believe you," and he said, "Do you have a Romeo? I could show you." I found a Romeo, and they did the fight. I'll tell you what's happened to him since then: National Youth Theatre, member of. I've seen him in a local production of *Of Mice and Men*. And three A-levels. A full intention of auditioning for RADA. And he was gorgeous as Tybalt.

Before I did the project, I had been known to a certain degree as very autocratic, slightly unbending. Although I didn't look on myself as being that, apparently that was the perception of me in the company. And I learned, slowly over the years, that if you were more flexible, more gentle, with authority, you could get more done. This was the thought, and I tried to instigate it. Got into *Ballet Hoo!*, proved beyond doubt that if your approach is correct, with compassion, love, understanding, you can achieve miracles.

I *know* I got this job because of *Ballet Hoo!* I was approached, and I said, "No, I couldn't possibly." Partly because I was reaching retirement age, I'd promised Denise we were going on a world cruise, I was really looking forward to doing the things that I wanted to do...that I thought I wanted to do. So they kept on at me for about three months until I...not because of what they said but because of what I'd thought: as I came close to retirement with BRB, I realized I did *not* want to retire. If I could have stayed with BRB, I would have stayed. That's why I accepted this job, (a) because I'm so interested in education, (b) because of my experiences with *Ballet Hoo!* I know I *can* communicate with young people, it's one of my strengths. And (c) because I don't want to stop. I just want to keep going as long as I possibly can.

I walked into a staff situation here which was set, although I did bring in a wonderful teacher from the outside, he used to be a principal dancer with the Royal Ballet, Errol Pickford. He was the only addition I made, and I'm thrilled to bits with him. So I had a fixed staff, but we have had many long discussions about the curriculum, about the method of teaching, the things that I expect the goals to be, and it's all being written down. Mary left me a curriculum, big fat thing, and I didn't really agree with all of it, so I gave each one of my staff a copy and I said, "I'd like you to spend the first term going over this, allied to your daily class, and [note] any questions you come across or any additions you think should go in. Then we'll get together in the second term, we'll go through it all, and we'll discuss what I feel about them and what you feel about them." Because I don't want my staff to feel that they have to teach something that they don't believe in.

Until they moved here [to Birmingham] four years ago, this was a dance school but much more, there was as much emphasis on West End production stuff, singing, jazz. Now it's a classical ballet school, so the emphasis has to be, through the curriculum, through the way we teach, on classicism. We also teach jazz, contemporary, flamenco, dance styles, all as part of the course. You know, these kids come in at 11 years old, Year Seven, they haven't formed physically or mentally by then. You take them on spec, you take them for what you see, what you hope for. Inevitably during the next three or four years, bodies change, approaches change, aptitudes for a certain style of dance change. So we have to give them the opportunity that if they do leave the school, having decided not to pursue a classical career, they have something else to...not fall back on, something else to fulfill their potential with. The jazz program in the school is absolutely brilliant. I've seen some of the kids in ballet class and some are more talented than others, as in all schools. Then you suddenly see these same dancers in contemporary or in jazz, and it's mind-boggling. And you can tell, '*This* is what they should do,' because they're putting everything, their bodies and souls, into this jazz.

I don't know what is most important for them, but I have to just think of myself. I didn't have any performance opportunity, born in the middle of Africa, so I think the most important thing for me was the broad teaching styles of the school I was at. Elaine Archibald had probably between 500 and 600 pupils at her school, an enormous school. And we learned tap, Scottish, ballroom—ballroom!—"mod-ren"...it wasn't called contemporary in those days but mod-ren...classical, mime, I can't even remember them all. *That* was the most valuable thing for me, I mean, proved years later. Glen Tetley came to the Royal Ballet, and he cast me in the first ballet he did [there], *Field Figures*. And I know I was able to emulate him showing the steps because of my background, because of what I'd been taught in Africa.

I'm not a competition person. I think they're ghastly, actually. If I see a competition as an entry into a formal education in dance, a way through, a breakthrough, if I see the prize as being that, then I'm much more tempted to [judge] it. And from a student's point of view, it's quite important to get the experience of being onstage in front of an audience. But the competition aspect of it I hate. In fact, there are some dancers in this world who are competition dancers. They go from competition to competition, and that's their life. Can you imagine being like that? It's awful. And too much emphasis is put on "I won the gold medal at so-and-so." It doesn't really mean anything in the end. All they do is endless *Don Quichotte* variations—this is not dance. And the applause that goes up when somebody does seven or eight pirouettes is just ghastly; it makes my blood run cold.

Now the most satisfying hat is…I can take you along the corridor—we have windows in all of our studios—and I'll show you the kids in there. Having a tiny hand, a tiny say in what happens to these kids' talent is the best hat to wear, the best, absolutely. Nurturing these kids through the next…I don't know how many years they're going to last, it could be a week…At BRB you take them in as young professionals and you start there, but this is different because of having the opportunity right from the beginning. This is actually much more dangerous and much more difficult, to take them in at this age and to be an influence on their careers from now.

I've asked myself about the future of ballet many times actually, and I can, given the right moment, get very depressed. Then when I'm in a better mood I can be quite positive about the future. Classical dance has lasted an awful long time and it's still going strong, in spite of my having said the audiences are the same. People do come and see it, people get an awful lot out of it. If we've managed to last this long, why shouldn't we last this long again? The world changes, but you still need…Diets change, but you still have to eat. And feeding of art will always be important. It doesn't matter what goes on around it, and possibly in the right way this may be part of saving this world of ours.

I don't know what to say I'm proud of. I'm just proud of being still here after 50 years. I'll stay in this job for as long as I have the energy to do it, as long as I feel I'm contributing something. And then, when I have to retire…Do I have to retire? I *don't* have to retire. I can do something else. I can do something else to do with dance.

Birmingham
November 2008

Jean-Pierre Bonnefoux

Jean-Pierre Bonnefoux (b. Bourg-en-Bresse, France, 1943) received his early ballet training in the Paris Opéra Ballet School from the age of ten. He entered the Paris Opéra Ballet in 1957 and achieved prominence and the rank of *étoile* in 1964 creating the title role in Maurice Béjart's *La Damnation de Faust*. Outside the Opéra, Bonnefoux appeared as a guest artist in *Swan Lake* and *Giselle* with the Bolshoi and Kirov ballets, in Roland Petit's *Le Loup* and Rudolf Nureyev's *Sleeping Beauty* at La Scala, as Balanchine's Apollo in Berlin, and with the Frankfurt Ballet and the National Ballet of Canada. After visiting New York in 1968 and 1969 to perform with his colleague Claire Motte, he settled there in 1970 when he joined New York City Ballet as a principal. He explored every corner of the company's repertory, from *The Four Temperaments* to *Bugaku* and *Liebeslieder Walzer*, and originated notables role in Balanchine's *Stravinsky Violin Concerto* (1972) and *Union Jack* (1976) before retiring in 1980.

§§§

Curious by nature, Bonnefoux was initially drawn to both acting and dance. Having ventured into teaching and choreography before he left France, he continued to investigate both disciplines while still performing, launching his American choreographic career in 1976 and teaching regularly at the School of American Ballet (1977–1984) and occasionally for New York City Ballet. In 1983 he took charge of the dance program at the Chatauqua Institution, a summer arts school, where he established a company for professionals in 1989. He joined the dance department of the University of Indiana School of Music in 1985, accepting dual responsibilities as the department's chairman and the student company's artistic director, and moved to Charlotte, North Carolina, in 1996 to direct the North Carolina Dance Theatre and its school. Undaunted by a heart attack in 2001, he still leads the respective companies and schools in Charlotte and Chatauqua.

§§§

You're making me think back. I don't go in the back of my life, so it's really strange for me. When I was almost ready to stop dancing...I don't think I planned anything, no. I thought about acting again, but if you feel that you have found your niche...I felt that dancing was really me, and the rest, the acting part, would have been outside the place that I was comfortable in and I felt I was becoming an expert in. And also, I really liked the idea that I had a lot to tell other people. And I always loved teaching; I started to teach when I was 18 years old, so the teaching part was something important. Also...It's strange, but it was important for me to finally be my own boss, I wanted to do things a certain way, and it was a chance for me to get started in that direction.

I had been with the best with Balanchine and Paris Opéra, the influences were very important, but what was important was who I was. If I was in Paris Opéra, if I was in New York City Ballet, I still wanted to do other things, I still wanted to see choreographers, I still loved more a small company than a large company. My favorite company was called Ballets U.S.A., of Robbins. It was a small group, and I saw them in Paris before I went to New York. I really loved seeing Robbins and his guys and the women, each of them had a face, very interesting. That's what was close for me to acting, and that's what I liked. So if you see me now directing a small company with eighteen dancers plus six from the junior company, it's because I see each one very strongly as one interesting person telling a story. And it was always like that for me, so I didn't change really.

The method of the Paris Opéra was that you stay there all the time, but some people had the possibility to do guesting outside, I had the possibilities to do that. So I went to the Scala and a lot of those places just because I had these chances. When you have the chance to dance with Carla Fracci, you don't want to miss that. Then I had the chance to work with Balanchine—you can't refuse it. So that's the way your life goes. So when I went to New York City Ballet it was not because I wanted to be in a big company—I'd done that already in Paris Opéra. It was searching for something, for some exceptional people [like] Fracci and other wonderful dancers, searching for the same standards basically. I think I had very high standards from the beginning, and so my searching was to meet the style of Balanchine and to meet the person, how is he doing all of what he's doing.

I don't remember ever having an opportunity that I wouldn't take, because I knew that it was going to help me to grow. I guess I believe in destiny also. Maybe I told you that when I was really young my mother, who was a stage mother, didn't know what to do for me at 14 years old—and *I* didn't know—if I should continue as an actor or continue in the Paris Opéra. So she went to see a psychic, without me but she brought a photo, and what he said was amazing. So then I knew that there were things that were already preordained. And actually, I'm curious. I'm still learning—I love to learn, it's really fun. I don't think it's trying to say I'm exceptional or I'm amazing. It's just that I'm curious, I want to know why something is happening.

But you know, there's one person that influenced me when I was young. He was a dancer in the Paris Opéra, known from insiders, like he was a dancer's dancer, but he never really became a big star. He was four years older than me and he had two names, Jean-Jacques Béchade and Jean-Jacques Delrieux; when he danced he was called Béchade. In Chatauqua now, where I'm still going for 27 years, one of the studios is called the Jean-Jacques Béchade studio. But what was amazing, in the Paris Opéra we all played chess, but he was the best one, no doubt. He was the best one at guitar but not just any guitar, he was the best one for flamenco guitar, with the soul. Jean-Jacques played, and he was going into his own world. When Balanchine choreographed, he was so into his own world that things would come out naturally. Jean-Jacques didn't even know, but he was basically living with meditation, he was so much in the present. So it seems that all my life I've been wanting to be like him, and it's only now that I'm far away from that that I'm meditating every day.

Around the early '80s, I remember there was a meeting in front of people, and Balanchine was asked, "So after you, what will happen?" which he did not like to answer, for sure. But he said something like, "Oh, Jean-Pierre and Peter have ideas," and he named me first. Isn't that interesting? So when I heard that, I thought maybe I could be the director of New York City Ballet, and for awhile I thought that sounded really good, and then Peter [Martins] is the one who got the job, and Balanchine did not decide that—it was done by the board. First, I didn't think I was ready to direct. Or I was too humble, I don't know what it was, or insecure, but I was not ready for that. And then I eventually realized that I really don't want a big company.

By the way, '79, '80, '82, '83, was the worst time in my life. We talked in '79? So I would say it started in '78. From '78 'til '80 I was struggling to be in shape, not to be injured, and then I had an accident in 1980 and it was really terrible, because I could never come back showing how I was as a dancer—I just was that guy who was injured. I was 36 when I stopped dancing, and I had decided to stop at 37 anyway—I would have danced one more year. I knew that at 37 I would teach and choreograph. I didn't know if I would direct but I knew that I would teach. But I wanted to have a good year and dance well, and I couldn't do it, and that was very, very hard.

I would have loved to do *Prodigal Son* and the Robbins *West Side Story* [*Suite*], which they did later, it must have been really fun. And I almost...I think I would have left the company around that time, even a little bit before, and I would have gone to work with Paul Taylor or with [Jiří] Kylián. Paul Taylor was already established; Kylián was, at that time, not that famous but he was magic for me. Kylián was the one that I admired, and he reminded me also of Jean-Jacques Béchade, he had his way of being and the creativity was sensational, the style, the flow of movement, the organic type of it...it was just divine. I was really tempted but I couldn't do anything because of the injury—that's what was so hard. It was a really bad year, the worst year. But as soon as I stopped officially my dancing career, I went for six months to classes at the Martha Graham school, I loved the formality of the style, it was wonderful. But it was just to learn it, not to perform, it was too late. And then our children came, so...

I was teaching already—it was a need. And I remember my friends were not supportive. They said, "But why should you become a teacher, when you should still be known as a dancer? People are going to think about you as already retired." But I needed to teach those guys, so it was 1975 when I started regularly at School of American Ballet. What happened was that I went to Lincoln Kirstein and also Balanchine eventually...I forget who came first, maybe Lincoln Kirstein because...we were not close but

I felt comfortable talking to him and I admired him. So I went to him and I said, "I would like to teach guys, because these guys... They work with the girls. They are ten or twelve years old, and I remember that I didn't want to work with girls at that age. We are not going to get dancers like that. You have to give them a class." And then I gave them four classes a week for seven years. The pay was terrible, but I just loved it—that was one of my favorite things in my life, to do that class.

I've had amazing teachers and I felt, and I still feel, that one of the most important things in life is communication. So there was no problem—I just knew I could communicate with those guys. There was really a need, for me but there was a need for the guys. Balanchine said or Kirstein said, "Do we have enough guys at that age?" I said, "Yes, there are seven guys." So I started, and there was something touching, something wonderful, it was like going back to the Paris Opéra when I was a student. And also I was treated terribly as a student, so I wanted to show those guys what a good teacher was and not the way I was treated.

The bad experience I'm talking about was when I was a little boy. From ten to fourteen I was in the school, and especially the first year...The teacher would give private lessons and my parents could not afford private lessons. I was maybe the only one who did not work privately with that teacher. So she wouldn't take care of me and she was very mean in class, and I would cry every day. But at the same time, just before her, my first three months at the Paris Opéra, I had a teacher [Monsieur Goudod] who was like your favorite uncle, so I had seen how wonderful a teacher can be. I was ten years old, and there were two exercises that I still remember. He was retiring, and he said, "Before I go, I want to give you two exercises that I think will be really good," and I'm still giving them—they're special exercises to prepare the feet, before the class. Nobody talked to the students when you're a kid. But he talked to us, he said, "I'm leaving and good-bye," and he was a good man. So when I started to teach, I'm sure, that struck me. And I was touched by those guys. I don't think I would have been touched as much in Paris, because in Paris...if you're a dancer, you dance. But in America, nobody accepted...It was tough for them, [to attend] the School. So I admired them and I loved to teach them and I had fun.

One of the seven was Peter Boal, so I was lucky. He was for sure a dancer. He would have danced anyway, but he said a few times—he was really very kind—that without these classes, he was going to stop dancing, because he did not want to be with the girls. So we had that camaraderie, but the only way to keep them interested was to change the steps every day, every time. So that's what I did. The guys would say, "Didn't we do that yesterday?" and I would say, "OK, so we'll do something more exciting." It had to be exciting.

I knew that there was not just one way to teach. I'd seen how Balanchine taught, I'd seen Paris Opéra, and outside Paris Opéra I had two wonderful teachers, an Italian teacher, [Raymond] Franchetti, and another one before Franchetti that was one of the best, [Serge] Peretti. They were very different. So there was no doubt that there was not one way to do things. You had to communicate with people, and if you want to reach them, then you need to find steps for each of them. And there was [Alexander] Pushkin in Leningrad that I loved also. He was one of the best ever teachers, he was the teacher for Baryshnikov and Nureyev, and [Alexei] Yermolayev was an amazing teacher. I wrote down so many classes, but I never felt the need to teach them exactly and to say, "I'm passing on tradition. That's the class from this teacher." It was much easier and a much better result to teach my own steps for these guys—I had to, and it came naturally.

Maybe I tried, at one point, to be teaching like these teachers, and then it didn't work, I couldn't do it. You have to be…not bright enough, but at least you realize you are not going to be like them at all. Also, because I was busy as a dancer, I did not have time to prepare. If I could have prepared the classes, I would have really prepared them like those teachers did. But most of the time it had to come from…Some classes, the steps come out a little bit like Balanchine, so I feel as though I have a connection at that moment with the spirit or whatever it is of Balanchine. It's just memories, maybe. I'm not saying the spirit is in me, but I'm close to those memories.

There was also in New York Stanley Williams, who from the beginning I could not understand, and I knew him from Denmark. I had taken classes with him, I had taken classes with his teacher, Vera Volkova. I remember at one point, because I thought tradition was so important, I said—in fact, it was not very nice—I said, "You are really teaching differently than Volkova." I was accusing him basically, saying, How dare you teach differently than your teacher? But he didn't take it that way. He said, "Yes, there's different ways to teach," and it was a really great lesson for me. So I had a lot to learn and I learned it from other people.

You know, it was a big change for me to dance in New York. After one year I remember saying to Pat [McBride, his wife], "I'm not really into the style. How long is it going to take me?" Pat said, "Maybe three years or five years," and I said, "I can't wait that long." It was really difficult. The musicality was very different, the attack...There was something at the Paris Opéra more about presenting yourself to the audience so they would look at you like they would look at photos. The positions were more important than the movement, and in Balanchine movement was more important basically than the positions.

For New York City Ballet, my teaching was not about helping them and correcting them: it was more to teach them a good class, and so it was almost like choreographing for me. Balanchine came one day, it was wonderful, and he gave me some good advice, how to use the pointework with the music, where the One is and the And is and all of that. That is very, very important and interesting, and I learned a lot that way.

My company I teach like once or twice a week, and it's harder now because the class is less important than it used to be. So what's hard is to motivate the dancers, professional dancers, to take classes seriously. I remember the first girl who told me something about that. She was in New York City Ballet, and I was telling her something in the class, and she said, basically, that she knows better what's good for her body. I'd never heard that before, but now you hear that all the time. So they do your class, but they also believe in what they know is good for them. It's not that they are going to change your class—you're the director, anyway—but...Like they do too much stretching now; for five minutes dancers stretch, I have no idea why, maybe it's because it feels good. So class becomes a place where you feel good or you warm up. It's not a place where you really learn something. It *is*, but there's a tendency to feel differently. It's also different...in my company anyway...no, in many companies...If you are in Balanchine's company, then you know what class you need to take, because of the repertoire and the style. Now it's different, many companies do so many different styles. So the class doesn't really serve their work with the choreographers. It's still a base but it's less important in a way.

I think I've simplified things now. Balanchine used to talk about the barre, that there are groups of steps, like almost families of steps—you do frappés with this, you do ronds de jambe with that—but that's all. When you are a young teacher, you have a tendency to want to choreograph or to make it really interesting or unique or intricate. Balanchine was one of the only ones—Stanley Williams also—who would do just simple steps but they would build something in that step, repeating the same step with the right energy, the right musicality. I think I teach more that way now, so my steps are more simple but I think they're more efficient.

I feel I get a lot out of the dancers and hopefully they get a lot out of me when I teach them, but what they do is so complicated now. Dancing is so much more complicated than it was 20 or 30 years ago. I would have loved to do what they do now, but I don't know if I could have done it. Do you know Dwight Rhoden? He's a choreographer in New York, he has a company called Complexions. He's the resident choreographer in my company and he does two or three new ballets a year with us, and there's an average of... let me see...maybe three movements a second. And he's not the only one—it's what's happening now. It will maybe look very old-fashioned one day, I don't know, but for the last ten years maybe... it started with Forsythe and it's still going on. I try to adapt the class, but it's hard for the dancers to adapt to another choreographer. When he comes he teaches some classes, and *his* class helps to prepare them.

In Dwight Rhoden's pieces or Alonzo King's—they're some of my favorite choreographers—there's not really a music that you follow. There's an impulse of your body that takes you, but it doesn't really connect with the music. So what's important to me is to remind the dancers that when they're doing some other styles that *do* connect to music, they better be connected. My thing is to make sure that the dancers use the music, that they...really *hear* the music, because they don't hear it anymore the way that we used to. I remember I saw...I forget who was the choreographer, but it was in Germany a long time ago and it was so funny. A wonderful symphony orchestra played Mahler or whatever, and the dancers had something in their ears like a Walkman, and they would listen to another music. During the ballet!

I like the result of three movements a second, it's exciting for the audience. Also, if we will do the same type of ballet...Most of the ballets for the last 20 years, except Balanchine, people won't want to see anymore, most of them are really passé. I mean, if you offer

200 channels to people, they don't want to go back to two channels. They want-to-go-to-the-next, they want-to-go-to-the-next, it's
a different thing completely. But in the studio if I see that a dancer
is missing this and this and that, then I do the class [to help] them
to keep those things. It's not about saving a tradition, it's about
serving them.

Everything goes so fast in America because the contract is so
short that we do a ballet so complex and the choreographer just
finishes two days before the show. And it's worse than it was ten
years, twenty years ago—the dancers have to do so many new ballets. It's hard to be a dancer now. They don't have enough time, and
that's the frustration as a teacher, that you wish you could spend
more time with them or the class would be two hours instead of one
and a half, but it's not possible. It's the money, that's a problem. I
mean, when I was in Paris Opéra...I rarely say "When I was..." but
I remember taking months to prepare for *Swan Lake*. But now, if
we will do *Swan Lake*, we have three weeks maybe—that's a lot—
to choreograph and to work on it.

But in class...When dancers don't know how to solve this problem or do this step, I'm good at figuring a way that helps them. And
what's good about that is then they don't lose confidence, because
it's very important that they have confidence in themselves, that
they know I trust them and I love them and have lots of affection
for them, and Pat is the same. As a dancer I didn't feel that confident. Pat was like a natural dancer but for me it was different, but
that was just insecurity, and there was nobody who could reassure
you or say you did well, there were almost no comments coming
from anybody.

Somebody in a college—he was a dean or something—said, "If
the only thing we teach them is self-confidence, we will have done
a great job," and I feel that strongly. I'm their support system. We
don't talk much about it, but they know that they can come to
me...I'm very sensitive to what they do, which is tiring, I get tired,
but I feel very much out of myself and toward them. I have to make
an effort not to do that too much, because otherwise I'm drained
completely.

You know, a long time ago people used to be in the same
company—I'm talking about business people—for 20 years, 30
years, that was the normal thing, and dancers too. Modern dancers...That was different, because there was not the money, but that
was the way we would think about ourselves, we always took it as

a full-time job. Somehow I knew dancing was going to be a very important part of my life where I would go on for a long time. But now I feel it's one of the phases of their life. It's their identity for now, but they are going to make money one day, they are going do computers, they are going to do other things, but not really teaching or choreographing. They give themselves maybe five years, ten years, dancing, I don't think more than ten years. For them it's a long time to do something, it's almost at the end of their...imagination, yes.

But also, it's harder than it was. I can see them getting burned out, and I would have been burned out with dancing three movements a second. And also...Around the country in general the dancers have a contract of between 30 and 40 weeks; 30 is not very good, 35 is OK, 40 is wonderful. So if you have a longer contract, then you have no time to think about something else, you're just completely involved with that. But if you have a 30-weeks contract, you have plenty of other time to *be* somebody else. So that changes you. Jacques d'Amboise said it was so hard when he stopped dancing because he was Jacques-the-dancer, that was his identity. But these dancers...their commitment is not the same as our commitment, and I think they can change identity much faster than the generations before.

In a way, what they do is much more abstract, so you don't see *them* as much. One thing that I love about my company, and in dancers in general, is the faces. For me, faces are the big thing. I want to audition somebody if I see a face, even if they're not perfect, but if you see the passion and that fire, then I want to work with that dancer. I've seen lots of shows—I won't tell you the companies—where I was not excited at all, where there's something neutral, something generic...They arrive on stage very often, and you don't see faces; that's the last thing you want to look at. You don't even look at the faces. And they don't want you to look, because they don't have that much to say with their faces.

Acting would be something that I wish we'd have time to do, but every time we have tried...We started in Chatauqua to do that, and there was no time. In Chatauqua it's seven weeks, part with my company, the [North Carolina] Dance Theatre, part with the Chatauqua Ballet Company. There's basically four different programs in seven weeks, so there's just too much to learn. Now it has changed from when I started doing 27 years in Chatauqua, but I felt and I still feel it's important to give them a chance to be onstage. What used to be—in summer courses generally, schools, anywhere, and even during the year—was basically, 'We cannot put them onstage because they're not going to look good, and we, the teachers, are not going to look good.' For a long time now the School of American Ballet is doing Balanchine ballets, and everybody thinks how great that is, but it was not like that everywhere and especially for a summer course [in] Chatauqua. Now everybody's starting to do shows during the summer. I don't say I was the only one to do shows, but maybe for a long time I was, because I think that is the best way to give them confidence, to develop them.

The best is for them to see that as a teacher you seem to know them better than themselves. And so you say, "You can do that." They say, "I can't," and I say, "Yes, you can go as far as that. That place is yours," and eventually you can bring them there, and at the end of the summer you see people have changed, because they were trusted to be in front of an audience. I think that's really big, and they're never too young to do that. You know, there are all those [arguments] that if you put them [onstage]...it's almost like those tap competitions, that the kids are showing off and it's not good, it's not classy. But I don't worry about classy or not classy. I have very high standards, so I don't worry to put them onstage, because I'm not going to give them something bad.

In my company, I want to choose a repertoire that's exciting for them and for the audience and for the choreographers. I love to see different choreographers, it's like at a dinner you want to offer the best food to your guests and I'm like that with my dancers. For example, can I tell you about one piece? A friend of mine went to a concert in Charlotte, and he said, "You should listen to this music." So I listened—it was bluegrass music, five musicians called Greasy Beans—and I said, "I really like this. We can do something on that." I gave the idea to a Canadian choreographer, Mark Godden, one of my favorites. The whole marketing [department], when they heard "bluegrass," they went into, 'Come on, you'll have fun,' and hand-clapping and all of that. But Mark Godden didn't get that message from me; I just wanted him to do what he wanted to do, and he did something really deep and pretty strong. So he finished the piece [*Double Blind*], and two weeks before the premiere we realized... The piece worked, but the marketing was the marketing, and we couldn't go back. It was out there, and people bought tickets to see that fun piece of bluegrass. So I told Mark Godden, "Your piece is not going in this program. We're going to do it, but in an evening called Dance Innovations that will be in two months. Are you OK with that?" And he was fine. OK. Now I have two weeks to find a choreographer.

So I received videos, I looked at them and got bored. So one day I said, "I'll do it," just like that. 'Am I crazy? No, I guess if I said it, I must know something.' I started to choreograph it, had a great time, and it became *Shindig*, something like Balanchine's *Western Symphony*. And then the marketing worked. We go on tour, everybody wants to see *Shindig*, we do it all the time, not because I want to do it but because it works. It's the biggest success for our company everywhere, I mean, on a program for kids, an educational program, everyone is having fun, and it's good for the dancers, it's good for pointework that we don't do that much.

You know, I choreographed something for my twin sister when I was five years old. So choreographing was always there, but somehow I've not gone as far in choreography as I could have, by laziness or I don't know what. Many times I almost found work on the side that I have to do so I couldn't prepare my ballet, and I would arrive at the studio without anything ready. I would even postpone it if I could, because…it's frightening. I still choreograph maybe once a year or once every two years, not much more. It's just something that I never trusted myself to do, it's as simple as that. If I'm pushed to do it, OK—you know, you do what you have to do when you direct a company.

But also I was 11 years in the university in Indiana, and for 11 years I choreographed five, six ballets a year, I didn't stop, and I think it was too much. It's hard to choreograph on students, it's not the same as professionals. The result is not as satisfying as when you see a mature dancer who takes over what you do. And I'm very…not difficult but…critical, so when I saw all of that, I said, "That must be me as a choreographer." I've done some things that I really like, it usually turns out OK, but lots of things have to happen for that. If somebody would give money to my company and say, "You have to choreograph," I will do it. And also, when I see that Alonzo King can do a ballet or Dwight Rhoden, I know that it's their life a hundred percent. It's not my life a hundred percent, so I almost feel like an amateur compared to them. That's their identity and…it almost did but it never became my identity.

It was a wonderful life in Bloomington, Indiana, it was great. I was the chairman of the department, we were part of one of the best schools of music in the country. But I felt that…again, I could stay there or I could go further in my life. That's my choice. But then I didn't know how to do it. So I went to see a motivational speaker called Tony Robbins. I saw him on TV in one of those info-commercials you see, usually at four in the morning. I was having trouble to sleep, I saw quite a few people who said, "I'm going to teach you how to do this, how to do that, you can do it," all those things. I didn't like the preachers, but that guy, I trusted him. He's 6' 7", he has a big face like a horse, and he's wonderful, he's positive. So I decided to go to see one of his talks and I thought, because it was on TV, that it would be a few hundred people, but there was 1,400 of us to see him. So the guy speaks for like eight hours, I heard all eight, it was amazing. I was not exhausted—I was captivated, I was excited, I had more energy than ever, and I felt he was talking to me. So I did all the exercises, and he really turned my life around. I realized that I didn't want to teach students only any more, I really wanted to work with the professionals. I knew that I had to find a way to get out of that situation, which was too comfortable. Why be so comfortable when there are more exciting things? I did not have the courage to do it, but he gave me the courage.

He prepared me, if I can explain it a little bit, with the way I would look at myself and the way I would believe in myself. I arrived in front of the board people, and I was…pretty good. I could see them being interested in what I was saying—I couldn't believe it—so I would go on, and then they would give me the job. I got three offers at the same time, and with Pat I chose Charlotte because it was like an ambitious new city where they would understand what I wanted to do, bringing choreographers, doing new stuff and having fun with that, instead of trying to bring tradition and saying, "I know *Giselle* and I'm going to do another version of *Giselle*." That would bore me to death.

That's a big statement and it's not really right, but things have changed and I think all the *Giselle*s and *Swan Lake*s should be just a small part of the rep. There's a very conservative audience all over America and you have to serve this audience if you have a company, and if I had a larger company we would do *Giselle* for sure. But the people that are always with the classical and the Romantic ballets…they will become old-fashioned. It's amazing how ballet is adapting. You know, if there would not have been somebody like Balanchine, I think ballet would have gone. That's my feeling, but maybe I'm wrong. But Forsythe was influenced by Balanchine, even Alvin Ailey was influenced by Balanchine, he talked to me about that. So there's always those people who influence you, and if you don't have these masters, the art form is finished. I really liked the idea of discovering talent, it was much more fun for me. I had tons of energy and I was ready to do whatever it took, I would work 12 hours or more. It was time for me to direct instead of being directed.

There was a nice company before in Charlotte, but it had to be rebuilt entirely. The initial challenge—I love challenges, I guess—was the idea that in America the symphony and the opera are king and queen or whatever you can call them; there's room for just two, and people want to be on the board of this and the board of that. But apart from New York, where you want to be on the board of New York City Ballet and Ballet Theatre, the ballet's always third or tenth or whatever, it's terrible. Very often, people don't really know about it, so it's like, 'Dance? I have to learn about dancing, all those guys in tights? Don't bother me with that.' When I arrived in Chatauqua, for example, there was no school, only a small, tiny little program. They wanted me because I had a name, but I don't think dance was part of the mission of Chatauqua. For some people dance was not American or dance is not the thing. So Charlotte was the same, the symphony, the opera, but the dance is not much. So I had to fight again, I just pushed, because I love this idea of building.

The privilege is to see the result onstage, definitely, to see dancers being transformed. And it's the idea that there's a new person who comes to see a show, never seen dance, somebody dragged them there—in America, it's really serious—and what the husband remembers is going to the recital of his daughter. That recital is the most boring thing he's ever seen, it's three hours long, he's missing a football game, and nobody tells him, "Oh, that's just amateurs, but professional dancers are very different." No, for him ballet is that stupid thing that he had to spend all that time watching and he almost fell asleep, he just went there to see that daughter and he barely could see her. So when that person comes, dragged, and that person says, "Boy, that's exciting," that's the privilege for me, to be able to expand somebody's horizon about dance as maybe different than what he thought it was.

The greatest obligation...oh, gosh, is just to be there, for the audience, the dancers, the staff, all day long, and to find solutions, to be creative, to be optimistic. You get the news that you had this amount of money for a program, now you have 70 percent of that money only. That's what it is to have a small company in America. And also the obligation is to be consistent; I'm often worried that we should never have one program that's really under our standard. I need to keep a certain standard, because otherwise people in the audience start to say, "This show is not as good as the one before." There's enough good choreography around to surprise them all the time and to make them say every time, "Wow, that was interesting."

Oh, the repertoire leads the audience—it [had] better. You can't really follow the audience. You have to do ballets that they want to come to, for sure. But you have to find a way that you are the one showing them what ballet is. I mean, next year we are going to do *Cinderella*. I choreographed it years ago, it's a good production, so we're going to do it again. I would prefer to do something more exciting to me, but that we have to do, and we have to do *Nutcracker* also. OK. But we have three other programs, and these are programs that I want to do, and I think they can feel the quality. The hardest is to bring them to the show. After they have come to the show...maybe I'm dreaming, but I'd say maybe 80 percent of the people want to come back.

Unfortunately, I think we're losing audiences from all the possibilities of those DVDs and iPods and all that, so that's why we have to do something exciting. I'm not saying we have to do what *they* want, because I don't think they really know what they want, and what's the point to see us if we show only what they like. So the whole thing is a balance, but the big news is that ballet can be very exciting, because it's live dancing and you see exceptional people onstage. I programed *Spartacus* one day and we sneaked in [*Chants* by] Alonzo King for the first time, on the same program, and a majority of people preferred Alonzo King to *Spartacus*. So we have a reputation now that people will be surprised by what they will see. Basically the message of our company is that ballet in general is much more varied and diverse than you think it is. Ballet is not just the stereotype—we're fighting the stereotype.

Charlotte is not a city where the people go to shows, but I know that when people come to see us, the ones who come back, who have a sense of our company, they *know* the dancers, and we try and promote them also. We believe they are stars, and the way we promote them in the ballets they really look like stars. So maybe that helps the people who want to see stars. I can't believe that some ballets are done with a corps de ballet where everybody has to look alike and imitate each other. I can't believe that some companies still are doing that, and then they hope that people are going to come back. It does not make sense for me, I don't understand that. I don't even like that idea of corps de ballet and stars. In my favorite company, that Robbins company, Ballets U.S.A., they were all stars. The rep was amazing, and the people...They were *people*, that's what I liked. I like the idea of a dancer being a person. When you see a company and each dancer is different, it's amazing.

Coaching is the crème de la crème, that's the icing on the cake. I have a friend who does not want to teach, she wants to coach, but unfortunately, that does not exist in America, just coaching. You have to teach for your career, even if you are a wonderful coach. It's just a few hours compared to many, many hours of teaching, but people don't have the time or the money to have a coach. Ballet Theatre had; New York City Ballet never had that. But coaching is extraordinary. You can pass on what you know and you can see it in a different light—what could be better? It's everything that you have done, that you know well, and you see it survive through that dancer, it's magic.

Pat and I have staged *Four Ts* [*The Four Temperaments*] for my company, and for dancers to get an idea of what Balanchine wanted, you have to know how to communicate so that they don't just do the steps. You don't need to tell a story of the step, but if you know how to motivate them and communicate with them, then it works. My ideas about Phlegmatic...Because I was an actor, I could really focus. That was the beginning of my meditation maybe, without knowing it. I just try to show them how extremely focused *Four Ts* is, how you get into yourself. That's something you can explain. And you see the result, and if it doesn't work—I can recognize it when I see them barely understanding—then you try it again, you try it again, and eventually you see a little light and you build on that.

When Pat staged *Agon*, she remembers it but there were some parts she didn't know, so she compared with somebody else who has staged it a lot and she looked at some videos. But video...It's like dancing without an orchestra. If you don't have an orchestra—which, for a small company, that's most of the time—it's just not the same thing. Oh, it's terrible, the tape is the same sound all the time, sometimes the sound is not very good, no musicians, it's hard.

So video is very dangerous. The dancers are not inspired, and the worst is when you're a young dancer and you learn through a video. If you're an older dancer, you already have an understanding and you know how to deal with things, but if you are a young dancer you just copy the thing like you would copy a text, it's terrible. I remember one day [years ago], I was walking onstage...I don't know if it was *Sleeping Beauty* or whatever, but my way of walking was imitating Rudi [Nureyev], and I didn't even know. Somebody said, "Why do you walk like that?" and I thought, 'Oh god, he's right. What am I doing?' Because what you can copy is the caricature, the bad part, that's all. The wonderful part of that wonderful dancer or actor or singer or musician...you can't do it. You copy what's really evident, the mannerism, and that's what's happening, I feel, with lots of dancers. They think they do a style, even Balanchine style, but if they learn it from the video, it's not the style that they learn, it's the mannerism, and it's a big, big difference. I've seen it in New York City Ballet, where I had never seen that before, people sitting in a studio looking at a video. I was surprised that it would happen there, but there's just not enough people who have worked with Balanchine, or I don't know what it is.

What's really wonderful in Balanchine ballets is that there's not just one version of it. I'm sure I did Phlegmatic in *Four Ts* pretty well, but I know that there's other ways to do it, for me but other ways for somebody else. So if I want to coach it with the idea that the person has to do it the way I did it and feel the way I felt it, that will never work. What's interesting is, How can that person get the same result of intensity, of focus, of...like rays of light coming out, *rayonnement*, radiance? How do you get the dancers to bring out whatever he or she has? Where do you find...the heart? Where do you find the heart?

I know that one gesture is not real and one gesture is real. There's an honesty of a movement, and I know I can recognize it because I don't like fakes. So I really like to see that it comes from deeper inside of them. One thing that's wonderful in the contemporary type of ballet is that it's not for the audience. The audience has to go into what the dancers do. There's not the question of classical projecting, selling, not that at all. There's 'Come to me. Come to me, because I can pull you into my world, and it's worth it.' That's how you see people who are in a group: some people, you are never going to follow. Some people, you just follow them and you think, 'What unexpected thing are they going to do?' That's what people want to know. They don't want to see the same thing that they can do. They want to be surprised.

You just need talented dancers who have a reverence for what they understand or what they learn about Balanchine. Karin von Aroldingen staged [Stravinsky] Violin Concerto in our company and I helped with that, and I don't think they were that interested in the fact that it was such an important ballet. They wanted to do things for themselves, put themselves in it, not to be in the shoes of somebody else, the invented clothes of somebody else, and that's what I respect. Pat staged Agon, then Karin did—at another time— Violin Concerto, and those two ballets felt right to the dancers every time, they thought they were done for them. Agon is just amazing, it looks like it was choreographed yesterday. Violin Concerto is the same story. There's a joy that comes out of Balanchine ballets, because of the musicality maybe, that carries you. And as a dancer that's what you want—you want to be carried.

My dancers had three and a half weeks of touring in North Carolina, with two programs, two or three hours on a bus, 15 cities. Often performing in the morning for kids, for the educational program, for schools, and then sometimes in the evening. We had an evening program and a morning program. What was great was that the Greasy Beans bluegrass musicians traveled with us, so at night they would play Shindig for us in the theatre. In the morning I'd give class every other day…Class is at 8:30 to 9:30, they dance at 10:00, then they dance again at 12:00, I mean, it's hard, and Shindig is not that easy to do. But because they trusted the music or trusted my steps, both together, it became something that carried them, and they did amazing shows.

For the evening shows, we had, for example, Twyla Tharp's Nine Sinatra Songs, Alvin Ailey's Night Creature, and [the concert version of] Balanchine's Who Cares? We call that American Masterpieces. Imagine! We don't have much money, but we can show this in small cities in North Carolina, and it's exciting for me to say, We're going to show you what dance is. One day the theatre was around a thousand seats, and there were 80 people, that's all. We started the show anyway, and they were the best, it sounded like it was full. It's very strange in North Carolina. Some cities, some towns, like the Outer Banks, have culture and they have artists and galleries, and [in] some other places those poor people have not seen anything. You listen to the radio and you just hear preachers, it's frightening, really terrible. So those 80 people had sort of a subscription for the shows, they wanted to see us, and they were clapping and having a wonderful time, and we were fine.

In my company, the dancers are so different that it really shows, and to do a good ballet, nowadays, I believe you need that diversity. Isn't it an example to the world that you should be diverse? When you see people doing ballroom dancing on TV, they could be from any countries. Art has no barrier, no boundary, no frontier. You can understand Chinese things, for example; it's not from your culture but you just have to look and then you get something. I think if we stay into ourselves we're going to be in trouble.

All those ballets from the past...I'm not so much into them emotionally so I cannot really talk about them, but in fact there's lots of people who like them. But the ballets that are done now...I think we really have to do some works that people can appreciate because of the music, because of the theme, because of the diversity of the dancers. You know, you see those big companies and you see just white people. But there's something there that's not right or so I feel, it's not normal. You cannot say, "One of the major art forms is ballet for white people." When you do things like that it's almost like digging your own grave. When I was young and I came to America, some of my favorite male dancers were Alvin Ailey dancers, African-American dancers, and I always felt that as a choreographer, I wanted to choreograph with them. So now, we have three African-American male dancers out of nine. One of them, an amazing dancer, made a comment one day which was interesting. He was feeling uncomfortable because it was after a show and we were looking for a restaurant. He was laughing and he made a joke, but it was a terrible joke; he said, "If you don't find me, look in the trees." When you go in certain places in America, there's all that history that's still around or you can see that it was there not that long ago. So I think that we have a duty in the arts to be more open, in ballet, for example, just with the type of dancers that we take and not ask them to look all alike. I don't want to preach, I don't want to say I'm right or you should do that. It's just my preference.

If you do something well, if you are in the flow when you direct, when you give advice to somebody, when you talk to the board of directors, then it's the best time. I don't think there is one thing that I prefer. It's wonderful to choreograph when you have a good day and it was wonderful to dance when you had a good day. I really feel that my job as a director is to do what needs to be done. So after my heart attack—oh, it was serious, five bypasses—I went back almost right away. There was no question. It was my company, I felt I had responsibilities. That's what I knew, that's what I loved. In my family nobody ever had a heart problem. Blood pressure was a little bit high for me. Cholesterol, I had no problem. So I took it as me not knowing how to deal with stress. I said to the doctor, "Could stress be the whole factor, the whole thing?" He said, "Yes." So that was another lesson to learn, that maybe I should do things differently. I still don't know how to do that, but if it's about stress, then I can do something about it. Bad stuff happens in life, but still you deal with it. It didn't cross my mind to stop.

I would like to have more money to collaborate with musicians and with artists, which really is very satisfying. We work with a designer for a new ballet, but if you have a small company you don't get that much design, because there's not money. But if you can have direct contact with some collaborators, that's what I hope I will develop. And also I believe that it's part of the success of ballet in the future, the ballet form, the contemporary ballet, to find ways like music did…Music is now taking influences from whatever countries they can find, and we haven't done that in ballet, we're really behind in that. There's nothing better to make you creative than to work with somebody else. And there's a tendency…Every day you have to do so much work that very often I don't really know what I did all day. I know I was there working, but it would take me at least half an hour to figure out what I did. But if we can step back and have other people in your life to influence you and help you, something comes out that you didn't know you had, and the audience is going to appreciate that.

You do also what will be possible. You have to go through grants…I'm realistic, so I know that you cannot just dream about this and this; you have to find ways to get there. For example, there's an indoor arena in Charlotte for 14,000 people. That's really where I would love to perform, because I know or I believe that if we can *get* there, people would really embrace what we do. Maurice Béjart was pretty amazing at bringing people together in an arena. He was not the greatest choreographer, he repeated himself so much, but I worked a lot with him, and it was amazing. In Venice...There was an evening, at midnight it started, with candles, and his company performed on two big boats put together on the canals, and people followed behind on boats—that was the show. I would love to do that one day with my company! So there are things we are not doing that we should be doing, [not] if you are Ballet Theatre or New York City Ballet, but all of us, the smaller companies, have to find ideas about collaboration and venues.

Maybe people should know that we are losing more and more really good dancers to Europe—I say that because I just lost one. The best ones or many of the most open ones are dreaming about Europe, and it's because of Kylián and Nacho Duato and Ohad Naharin, all those people. There's something in the freedom that the choreographers have, they have more time to work...If you are a dancer from Ballet Theatre or New York City Ballet...I'm not sure that those are the most open dancers, but it's easy to stay in those companies, so you don't even have to open your eyes and look. At Paris Opéra, people started to open up when Nureyev was there. He chose some amazing young dancers from the corps de ballet instead of the older stars, and then directly the company changed and the rep changed. But the dancers that I see or that I know or I hear of in many other companies, they dream of Europe. And if the dancers dream about something else, it's not that great for us. You know, they could go to Europe and not like it. That could happen also. But how can you resist a 52-weeks contract? Our contract is 34 [weeks], 36 if we are lucky. Next year I don't even know, maybe 32. So it's very hard. One dancer who left and is coming back—that does not happen very often—is going to another company in America, because that company offers 44 weeks. If they really want to dance, they don't want to dance 30 weeks or 32 or 34. They want to dance more and be paid.

You can't stop it. But, for example, we did over the last few years two ballets of Nacho Duato, and that was very exciting for the dancers and also for the audience. We did one piece of Forsythe and we have to do it again. But the music was pretty loud and not very good for the American [taste], and people on my board said, "I don't like loud modern music. Forget about it." Somehow I pushed for it, for the Forsythe, and it was *loud*, really terrible, and then at the end of the show everybody stood up and they were clapping and going crazy. In Charlotte! So that shows me that they have it in

them, but I don't think they let themselves...Americans in general...
I don't know if I should say it, but many people don't know how
to accept to be moved by the arts. It's almost something you don't
do, so we have to be even more inventive or creative. These are the
problems; when you look at the whole picture, that's the big worry.
So I'm just hoping—I'm an optimist anyway—that the government
will realize that they need to support the arts at the state level and
federal level. It's really important that people...not just feel something but show that they feel something with the arts.

A big company? That's not me. No, not at all. I want to make
sure that I'm with a group of people where I know each of them
and I can talk to each of them and I can help each of them, so it's
personal. We have a real contact together, maybe not as much as
I would wish but there is something easy between us, and I don't
believe you can do that with a big company. We're eighteen dancers plus six dancers from our second company, 24, let's say 30
maximum. My dream is for us to be the best company in America
of this size—that's really what I want. There was a collaboration
[under discussion] between two companies when I started, but
the other director [Robert Weiss of the Carolina Ballet] wanted
to have more dancers and do bigger productions, and I thought,
'Oh, gosh. No thanks.' So I try to find ways to go forward. I was
given so much, to be with Paris Opéra and New York City Ballet,
that in a way it would be satisfying enough, for anybody I think,
to be just talking about that, bringing that forward, all the time.
But, you know, I was always different. I always wanted to do
some other things.

New York
April 2009

David Wall

David Wall (b. London, England, 1946; d. London, 2013) received his entire training at the Royal Ballet School, which he entered at the age of eight and left nine years later, graduating into the Royal Ballet touring company. He was promoted to soloist in 1965 and to principal, then the youngest in the history of the Royal Ballet, in 1966. By the time he transferred to the parent company at Covent Garden in 1969, he had already established a reputation as a danseur noble, having partnered Margot Fonteyn, at her request, on several tours. Equally at home in the nineteenth- and twentieth-century classics, he possessed a remarkable gift for dramatic roles, which led to notable successes in de Valois' *The Rake's Progress* and Balanchine's *The Prodigal Son*. Following his 1970 debut as Romeo, he created Lescaut in MacMillan's *Manon* (1974) and Crown Prince Rudolf in his *Mayerling* (1978) before retiring from dancing in 1984.

§§§

As soon as he left the stage, Wall joined the Royal Academy of Dancing as associate director; he became its director in 1986 and remained in that position until 1991. He then spent several years freelancing as a teacher at home and abroad before concentrating his experience and skill on English National Ballet as its ballet master (1995–2007). A governor of the Royal Ballet companies from 2007 until his death, he was also teaching regularly at ENB when we met in the company's headquarters to catch up.

§§§

I wasn't hooked until I was working with John Field, the director of the touring company, and he gave me a love for the theatre and acting. He had assisted so many great artists, as opposed to just dancers, that that's how he brought me up as a dancer. He encouraged me to go to see theatre performances, and he also allowed me the space to explore roles. Because we were in a touring company, dancing an enormous amount of ballets and an enormous amount of performances per week, I was perhaps doing *Swan Lake* twice a week, *Fille Mal Gardée* twice a week, so one got a lot of work under one's belt in a very short time. But it also gave me the opportunity from night to night to be diverse and play with the roles and all of the standard classical works.

That was the advantage of performing within a repertoire company that was doing eight shows a week. It was like putting an overcoat on every time you did a role, it felt comfortable, and the nervous adrenalin was there but it wasn't nervous-scared. Comfortable means looking forward to doing it, rather than fearing it. You know, certain roles one feared in one's career—I used to fear *The Dream*. No, I didn't fear it, but it was something that I didn't feel fitted me. I was at a stage where I could have quite easily said, "I don't want to perform the ballet anymore," but I remember Rudolf [Nureyev] saying, "If you do that, you'll be on the slippery slope." So I maintained my performances of Oberon for years and kept my mouth shut, and as lovely a ballet as it is, I didn't enjoy any of them.

The mentors I had when I was training latterly...There was a ballet that John Cranko created that was very male-orientated called *Antigone*, and of course David Blair creating [Colas in] *Fille Mal Gardée* and Rudolf coming to London. Those were enormous influences. And the other two influences I remember very much as a student were the Russian companies coming to Covent Garden. We didn't work with the companies, but I remember seeing performances of Ulanova and [Nicolai] Fadeyechev, [Yuri] Soloviev, [Vladimir] Vassiliev. Then Christopher Gable had an enormous influence on me as a youngster, to see the way that he interpreted roles. He and Rudolf were ahead [of me] and very different. Christopher could bring anything to life on the stage, which was marvelous—his Act IV of *Swan Lake* was absolutely fantastic. I think when he created his ballet company [Northern Ballet Theatre], that's an area that he wanted to bring to the fore, that ballet was theatre, it wasn't just pyrotechnics within a story. And Rudolf had a charisma that one wanted to emulate. But in fact, if there was one artist in the world that really influenced me, it was Paul Scofield. Everything he did on the stage, one really believed in, and his general intensity of performance was something I very much, probably subconsciously, wanted to bring to what I was doing. You're so involved in steps, but being in the touring company when we were performing in the provinces, or the regions as we're allowed to call them now, one almost got to a state of getting bored with roles because you were doing them so much, so you had to bring other things to it.

Since I gave up dancing, *Mayerling* and *Manon* seem to be the two roles that everybody remembers me in—Kenneth always managed to make me into a sort of anti-hero. But one challenged oneself so much in those years to actually establish the male dancer in all the standard classical roles, one really put oneself out to try to make them real and alive. Then suddenly you're cornered into *Mayerling* and *Manon*.

I now realize *Mayerling* was a huge part of my career, because after creating something like *Mayerling*, it's very difficult to imagine creating anything quite as big. I'd had a spate of injuries five years prior to my retiring and when I stopped I was very fit, just age was creeping up. I was having to put a lot of time into roles like *Sleeping Beauty*, which I used to virtually get out of bed and dance, and a huge amount of effort, physically, into maintaining the sort of standard that one wanted to maintain—I used to keep well away from ever seeing myself on video or film. When you're dancing at Covent Garden you're not dancing that often, and the knowledge that we had in those days about maintenance and diet, even though it was only 25 years ago, wasn't as great as it is now. So...it wasn't a struggle, but I was having to put a lot more energy into the physical side of things, prior to even getting into class.

I was quite lucky in the fact that Freda [Alfreda Thorogood, his wife] had retired three years before me and she'd done the Professional Dancers' Teaching Course at the Royal Academy of Dancing, through a great friend of ours, Alan Hooper, who was then directing the Royal Academy of Dancing and encouraged her to take that role. She was—she still is—*such* an amazing teacher, and I was consciously sort of assisting her during the course of her learning the process of teaching. It was then that Alan Hooper invited me onto the executive committee, whilst I was still a dancer, and I suddenly realized that the teaching of ballet was probably the most important thing of all as far as youngsters are concerned, and that [the RAD] was an institution that was responsible for a great deal and that teachers needed to teach youngsters safely...I'm talking about real beginners, sort of six years old.

There were areas within the Royal Academy of Dancing system that needed re-looking at, and Alan took it on board that changes should be made. He was basically trying to bring the Academy into the twentieth century—not the twenty-first, the twentieth century—because the organization was steeped in rather old-fashioned ideas and run by people who probably weren't very aware of what was happening in the profession. The profession and the training at the Royal Academy didn't seem to run parallel. Alan started by changing the content of the major syllabi—I wasn't involved in the nitty-gritty of it—and that in itself was a six-year process from beginning to end. In fact, one of the frustrating things about working with the Academy was that everything took so long. It being a worldwide organization, it was always hard to get anything done.

From my point of view, there was no continuity within the work from one grade to the next. One isn't trying to make a ballerina out of each and every child starting at the age of six, or I think pre-primary is actually five. But still, you have to have a line that's going to bring them up to the age of ten when they know how to point their feet and how to use their port de bras in a very basic way and how to find rhythm. That's why the new syllabus incorporated free movement, almost a eurythmic type of movement. Prior to that, you had nice little dances like the Birdcage Dance that the children performed at the end of each grade. But there was little continuity or build-up, and while I'm not talking about serious ballet build-up, I'm talking about children just being educated in movement, rhythm and the fundamentals of dance and music.

I worked through the old, major RAD syllabus at the Royal Ballet School...I don't know whether my teacher at White Lodge, Sarah Payne, was an RAD teacher, but we always used to do RAD classes. The value is...it's like Bournonville or Vaganova. You've got something to gauge things against, a sort of leveling thing. You forget about it quite quickly when you become a professional dancer. I always said to Alan, "The thing about the RAD is that you learn it as a child and it's quite responsible for how you end up as a dancer. Then you become professional and forget about it. And then at the end of the career a lot of dancers come back to the RAD."

Two years before I gave up [dancing], the chairman of the Royal Academy had actually offered me a position, whenever I wanted to take it up, as director, and Alan Hooper had invited me to New Zealand to teach on a summer school. I didn't do a teacher training course. The one that the RAD did actually gives you the technique for teaching, and it cuts in half the time that you'd have to learn by trial and error. But I was always fortunate in having teachers during my career that really helped me. One was Erling Sunde, and the other was Terry Westmoreland. And there was Brian Shaw, who was a teacher in the Royal Ballet. So I had three people that really made me conscious of finding dancers' physicality and creating a class that is right for the body, not just a syllabus class or a set of exercises to go through. I always used to work extremely hard in class as a dancer, in a very disciplined way, and I rarely didn't do class, because I felt that my physique needed to work continuously. Therefore I took on board a lot of work that these teachers were offering me as a dancer, you know, it gets stored away in that memory bank. Erling Sunde was a very stable teacher, he used to teach the same barre virtually every day, which could get slightly monotonous, but it was such a good barre you felt physically right when you got into the center to start doing any pyrotechnics. And Terry Westmoreland had worked with Vera Volkova, so I think probably Erling and Terry gave me subconsciously quite a lot of Vera's work.

I was teaching professionals in New Zealand, because there was a professional level to the summer school, and I remember coming back and everybody saying I was dancing so much better. I wish I'd started teaching when I was 20, because it makes you very aware that what comes naturally isn't natural to everybody. To try to pass that on...It's an amazing career, teaching, that can be very frustrating but at the same time, if there's an element of success in the pupil or the dancer, it's really rewarding.

I was offered the directorship of the Academy...Actually, my farewell performance was sort of two months after I'd started at the Academy. I was assistant [director] for two years, I think. I had Julia Farron as the artistic director, Priscilla Yates as the special projects director, and Donald Scrimgeour was the administrative director. Alan's death was very sudden, and when Alan died, that's when the position was offered to me.

It was quite an eye-opening experience. I learned a great deal about publicity, about organization, about planning, through Priscilla and Donnie. One taught summer schools, I taught the Professional Dancers' Teaching Course now and then. The pleasurable times were the summer schools and creating anything new like the children's syllabus, which was probably the most important. I helped create correspondence courses in anatomy for dancers and the history of ballet, collated and worked with the Surrey University to get the history side of things organized…Being a worldwide organization, we were trying to standardize the world as far as their knowledge was concerned but not giving them any information as to how to do it. So we started these correspondence courses, which in itself was a headache, whether to translate them into Mandarin or Cantonese, all of that sort of thing. It was a vast organization, nobody realizes the size of it.

When I stopped at the Academy, I gave myself a breather and then started freelancing as a teacher, basically in schools with young students. Teaching students is a great leveler. If you're standing in front of a company, you're not having to teach them what an entrechat six consists of or why they're falling over…well, you have to for pirouettes and things like that, but you're not starting over from the foundations. I never taught tiny babies, but I taught ten-year-olds upwards, and it was quite hard. You have to be such a psychologist, if that's the right word, in getting youngsters to learn. You've got to give them the amount of technical information along with an area of fun along with an area of musicality, and basically they've always got to go out of that class having enjoyed it. So that was really hard work. You have to work week by week by week to build to a certain level.

I tend not to be too politically correct when I'm teaching. You need to touch a dancer's foot, for example, especially with youngsters, to make them feel where they want to find the arch and things like that. And there has to be an element of discipline. That's what's great about youngsters who do dancing, that they *do* have that discipline, but it's something that is probably alien to them in their other classroom situations. There's no way you can conduct a class, either of students or professionals, unless there is discipline there, and that's what I try to do. I set out the goalposts when I first start teaching a company. I'm happy for there to be an element of communication amongst themselves; I don't mind if they're talking as long as it's not disrupting other people. And I like them to laugh and I like to laugh with them, but at the same time they've got to be doing their work properly. Otherwise they injure themselves, it's that simple.

What actually got me back into teaching was working with the Remedial Dance Clinic in Harley Street, with Shirley Hancock and Justin Howse. Justin was an orthopedic surgeon. Shirley was my physio for years. I think it was Ros Whitten who had a very bad back injury that kept her off for months and months, and Shirley said, "Would you mind having a look at her?" So I started teaching remedial ballet classes, starting them back on the road to recovery. I knew a lot from my own injuries and recovering from them. I'd also organized with Shirley this correspondence course on anatomy for the dancer and I'd worked with both Winifred Edwards and Joan Lawson, who taught me when I was coming back from injuries. So I had all of that experience and I worked initially with Shirley, in the same room.

My way of thinking is that there are only two reasons for injuries: there's traumatic injury and bad technique. There's not much else. You can't do much about the trauma of falling downstairs or getting run over by a bus, but technique weaknesses can often create the injuries. When a dancer's working really hard, the only reason they injure themselves is if their brain sort of slips for a few seconds, through fatigue. Probably too little work is worse for a dancer than too much. I always find that the harder the schedule… It's got to be a measured schedule, you've got to adjust very much what they do during the day, but the more performances a company is doing, the better.

I did my freelance teaching at three schools, they were my mainstays. I went to London Studio Centre, to Rambert and to…I think it was called the West Street School, where Volkova had been. Natasha Lisakova ran it. Julia [Farron] was there after she retired from the Academy, Maryon Lane taught there, I used to teach the boys there. I was doing remedial stuff when needed. I had a wonderful week; I used to work Monday, Tuesday, have Wednesday off, teach Thursday, Friday, which suited me very well. But then the diary got a little fuller. Harold King invited me to teach his company, London City Ballet, which I did for a few months in London. Then I suddenly realized that actually that's the thing I was really enjoying, working with professional dancers. Not that I wasn't enjoying the rest, but it was a preference because…I'd done my schooling.

Then Derek Deane invited me here as ballet master; he'd just taken over the directorship, after Ivan Nagy. I didn't know whether I wanted something quite so permanent, because I felt that if you're going to be a ballet master with a company, you've got to be A Ballet Master and be there morning, noon and night. But anyway, I admired very much the direction he wanted the company to move in and that he wanted to get an established style for the company. So after ooh-ing and ah-ing I said, yes, I'll do it.

It entailed teaching and it entailed rehearsing and it entailed discipline of the company, certainly amongst the boys. I said I didn't want anything to do with the administrative side of things, but obviously there was the casting which I was involved in with a group. That was what was so good about Derek: he got people together and worked with them very well as a group. So that was my thought of what the ballet master should be. There wasn't anything that threw me.

I remember Julia Farron talking to me, before I'd really started to teach, and she said, "Teaching's actually like performing, because you have to put on a performance for your class," which you do. That doesn't mean to say that you're actually performing the steps, but...For example, working with English National and virtually giving them class every single day for the last ten years, you come through those doors and you can't allow them to know that you're not feeling like doing it, which often you aren't. Teaching a company, you're very much responsible for setting the whole pattern for the day's work by what you do with the hour and a half you have with them. You often have had a bad day the day before, but you still have to come in and say, "Right, everybody, let's go."

You have to know what their daily schedule is, how hard they're going to be working, as a company or as individuals within the company. You've got to know what types of ballets they're working on—you maintain their classical technique if they're doing a lot of contemporary work, but you realize that they've got to have a little bit more freedom in the exercises they're doing. I teach very differently when they're performing [and not] just rehearsing, the class is more intense. Then you have to be aware of individuals who are doing roles that push them technically; you might give them combinations—sometimes they don't even know—that they're going to need to do two hours later. You have to prepare a class. You can't just walk in and begin. You *can*, I mean, I once could—don't know how well I could now—but you have to take on board the whole feel and mood of the company. Sometimes when they're very tired, when they're at the end of the year or doing a big Albert Hall season, which is tiring for them, that's when you bring in the humor side and you just lift them up and have a laugh. You have to do so many different things to get, hopefully, the best out of them. And some dancers respond to you, and some don't.

I actually think that the whole emphasis of dances and dancers has changed slightly over the years since I started performing. Not the emphasis...the mentality of dancers has changed somewhat, because everybody is so much into the pyrotechnics of the art form. I think they need to be, it's essential, but often the audiences are demanding the pyrotechnics at the expense of the artistic side of roles. Ideally you have to have it all. I suppose throughout the history of ballet some people have been better actors than others or better dancers than others. But it's important to cast dancers correctly, and perhaps the weaker dancers...I always think that a weaker dancer who has a good acting ability can bring up the level of their dancing, and often an excellent dancer who's a bad actor probably...will still be a bad actor at the end.

When I was creating roles, Kenneth's roles for example, the linchpin was the period and how you would behave within that period. You virtually had your hair cut the way [the characters] used to have their hair cut. I remember with *Mayerling*, I spent hours with Nico [Georgiadis, the designer], organizing from act to act the time difference and what [Crown Prince Rudolf] would look like; you know, he had different beards and different styles of hair [in each act]. Nico and I actually talked about that, which I think a lot of dancers now maybe wouldn't even consider.

With the princes, certainly from the boys' point of view, there's the emotion and the fact that they are portraying live characters that are dancing within whichever period the production's set in. The prince in *Beauty* and the prince in *Lac* are very different, again depending on the production, but one's sort of gothic and one's a sort of Renaissance [figure], and you therefore...And *Giselle*, there's Albrecht, different again, and it's not just a question of doing the steps. I never wanted to be known as David Wall doing Albrecht, I wanted people to believe it was Albrecht, it's that simple.

It's the way that they're taught the roles initially that's changed. Whereas nowadays a young dancer can pick up a video of Natasha [Makarova] doing *Swan Lake* and school herself in that way of doing *Swan Lake*, in our day we couldn't do that at all. It had to be passed on through word of mouth. You get a preconceived idea from the video of what the role is about, rather than you discovering what the role is about—that's where I feel it tends to go wrong. There was one ballet I learned from a video, which was *Voluntaries*. We didn't learn it, but Glen [Tetley] showed us the video, which I found enormously inspiring to watch. But then, when trying to work on it, I always had in the back of my mind this image of somebody else doing it. And it's not the same as seeing somebody else performing it, because that's live. Video's a great record for the ballet master, but when I went to Hungary to put on *Mayerling*, I specifically said, "I don't want you to watch Irek [Mukhamedov] and I don't want you to watch me on the video"—the two of us were very different in the role—"I want you to actually bring yourself to the role. So don't drown yourself in the image of somebody else doing it, because you try subconsciously then to replicate what you've seen."

At ENB...well, basically they work with never enough staff to spend time...If somebody was going into a role, not a principal role obviously, we'd go, "Watch the video." Sometimes the videos are so bad anyway, they could only see the steps. They can see whoever they want to see nowadays on the video, and they always aspire to guest artists that come and work with them here. But now... It's so much free-er as far as expression is concerned. Not expression, but it's so much free-er now as far as dancers moving around from country to country, from company to company. Productions move...I don't know what the result is. My initial feeling is that everything gets slightly watered down. You get wonderful dancing, and probably you get wonderful, wonderful interpretations... but rarely. I don't know, it might just be me getting...What are we called? Grumpy old men. I've never been grumpy.

I've adored the dancers in this company and I've adored their different personalities. I think they work exceptionally hard, probably harder than we did. They have more awareness of their physicalities and how to get the best out of their physiques—we're talking about the intelligent dancer. They have been given information which the majority of them have taken on board, certainly as far as their physical well-being is concerned. I think they're very lucky. They get more than we got in rehearsal inasmuch as rarely does a principal cast go onstage in this company without having a stage call. But we didn't. I never had a stage call, not with lights and things, for lots of productions. You got an indicated set, but you never got an orchestra. A lot of them get...not necessarily orchestra [rehearsals], but they get well prepared before they go on. Often in our situation if you were second cast or something, you had to prepare yourself, especially when a ballet was being created. With *Mayerling*, Kenneth hardly allowed anybody into the studio who was a second cast, which was hard.

What actually gave me the inspiration to be generous with my information to other dancers was the fact that David Blair helped me with *Fille Mal Gardée* and Christopher and Lynn [Seymour] helped Freda and me with *The Two Pigeons*. They coached us in it, not for a great length of time but they spent time with us talking, voluntarily, in the studio, and passing on their love for the roles and their approach and what Ashton wanted. So to me it's an automatic thing to pass it on. I remember rehearsing David Peden in *The Two Pigeons*, not officially but sort of seeing him working the role, and certainly I worked with Stephen Jefferies and Wayne [Eagling] with *Mayerling*. A lot of people can bring different thoughts to roles, which I think is their privilege to do, as long as one's not moving away from the concept the choreographer had.

It's easier to pass on the MacMillan rep in a way, because somehow they're all real people, he always utilized real personalities in his choreography. None of Kenneth's work has to be totally stereotyped. So they'll be passed on the way the Diaghilev repertoire's been passed on. There'll always be somebody around that remembers either what I've said or what Lynn's said. But I think the ballets will hold up anyway, certainly MacMillan's, because they're not as ephemeral as some other ballets; there's something very stable there, because often the storyline's so solid and human. Kenneth never detached his ballets from life.

I thought [Johan] Kobborg was absolutely splendid in *Mayerling*, really sensational. I didn't work intensively with him, but seeing him onstage there were moments where I could say, "You know, the way you're walking in this scene doesn't look true to what else you've done." It's very easy to be melodramatic in some of Kenneth's roles. Less is more sometimes. That's how I used to feel. Acting on stage is as much a technique as dancing, and if you feel that you've got to project an emotion, fear or anger, and if you think too hard about projecting it, it becomes false. Sometimes it's best just to let it happen, as long as the thought's there. Certainly when we televised *Mayerling* for the South Bank Show, I was conscious that there were going to be cameras...you knew you had three viewpoints that were capable of getting very close. So I had to change my whole way of performing; I was aware that I couldn't do the role the way I did it on the stage.

For the stage it has to be larger than life. This is what was great about being in a touring company working in a different theatre each week, the fact that each theatre was a different size. So you could be in an intimate, 700-seater one week, the next week you're in a 2,000-seater, and you had to adjust the way you got across to the audience. Nowadays, because they don't [tour] often enough, that doesn't happen. Except, you see, with this company—the way they perform at the Albert Hall is amazing. It *is* huge but it's not huge, in a funny way, because the audience...Although you might be really high up, you're not miles back.

Over the years I've imagined performances that I've seen of artists and companies, and they're so much better in my imagination than seeing them again on a film. Sometimes if I see Margot [Fonteyn]... she was probably the worst dancer ever to put on film, because she was so involved in carrying the audience away, so she's not the right person to be talking about. I remember seeing Lynn in *Romeo* the very first season they were doing it, long before I did it, and it made *such* an impression on me. That's what suddenly made me understand what true artistry was about. I wasn't even conscious that she had pointe shoes on. Every line she made wasn't like an arabesque, it blew my mind away. Things have moved on in some very good ways, technically and aesthetically, in dancers today, but it's a thing of what's in vogue. Freda and I have recently been trying to get some of our videos transferred to disk and have therefore been watching some old productions we were in, and we go, "Oh, my goodness!" Some of it wasn't wonderful technically...but audiences still loved it. A ballet audience is a dreadful audience really— I'm talking about an uneducated ballet audience—because...Ballet is not like singing. If somebody's singing out of tune, then virtually the whole world will know it. If they're dancing not quite so well but now and then put in some sensational movements, you can get away with it.

It's very interesting. Nowadays that might well play a bit more of a part than it used to, because if you do a spectacular manège now, the dancers expect the audience to applaud and often they do. In our days...It was really only Baryshnikov and Rudolf who started that sort of audience participation in their work. When I was performing I wasn't conscious of the audience. I was [only] conscious of whether the theatre was full, fingers crossed. With something like *Two Pigeons*—which I adored to perform—you knew within the first three minutes how the end of it was going to be audience-wise. There were certain humorous things that one had to get going, and if you managed to do it within the first three minutes, then you knew that things were going to be all right. With Kenneth's works...Certainly with the creation of *Mayerling*...I used to create for the choreographer rather than the audience. It didn't worry us too much whether it was successful as far as the audience was concerned. It was always wonderful if the audience loved it, but if dancers know they're on [form] that night and they're doing a lot of pirouettes, they're going to be happy bunnies. If they're off, they're off. Again, an audience probably can't tell. I don't think they can tell the intricacies of the pyrotechnics. They can tell how high someone is jumping and how fast or how many times they're spinning. That's why these young choreographers are so silly; they rarely repeat a step more than twice, and you need to repeat at least three or four times before an audience can take in how difficult the step is.

It was quite something when Glen came in and started working with the Royal, quite frightening. There wasn't an injury factor. It was just sort of...trying to create a different technique. Nowadays dancers do that automatically, take on board different techniques. I think they have probably explored more types of dancing than we ever did, in their choreographic output as students and the fact that they probably have all done contemporary work as students. Contemporary and modern ballet are far more on their wavelength than they ever were on ours and more often on their plate, and they're very much more flexible, mentally and physically, then we were. It's like when Kenneth put on *Song of the Earth* in Paris: a lot of the soloists refused to do it, because there were movements that were actually turned in. They had a great battle. But now you can get a choreographer like Wayne McGregor coming in to work with Tom and Ag [Thomas Edur and Agnes Oaks], and that's a very different way of moving. I think initially it was a struggle, but then they got on his wavelength and it worked very well. And they're far more open than we ever were, because they're more exposed to these different types of techniques. That's not to say we weren't trying to explore different ways of working. I mean, that's what Kenneth was good at. He wanted us very much to explore movement that sometimes was impossible. If he wanted us to be doubled over with our leg thrown around our ear, we'd just say, "I'm sorry, Kenneth, but that actually is not physically possible," and he'd say, "Well, thanks for trying."

If one's wanting to get a company look, which I think is quite important for any large company that are doing the classics, certainly it can be quite hard, not necessarily for us as ballet masters but for the dancers. I find this especially if they've been trained in Russia or in the Russian school, the Vaganova school; they tend to think that is the only way of working. I'm not saying it isn't—it is *a* way of working—and sometimes it can take a long time for them to be less rigid in their mental outlook. If you've got a corps de ballet [dancer], there are certain times when they can't do an arabesque, perhaps, the way they were asked to do it in Spain or Cuba. But then, that's what the rehearsal process is about, but you can see sometimes that they do have a struggle. I always used to say to them, "We're not saying what you learnt is wrong, but we just need it to be like this at this stage."

I think it's very important to have a company style. I think it's very important to have a company repertoire. The identity of companies is no longer there, because every company's doing every ballet that was ever created—with Kenneth's works, they do them all over the world. Which is great, but one of the fortes for the Royal Ballet was that they had a repertoire that nobody else did, so they could tour the world and the countries they were touring to had not seen those ballets before. Now there's a great comparison between one production and another, which I'm not saying is a bad thing, but you need to define a style. The *Manon* that ENB are doing, it's got a different design, and sometimes if you're a purist, you see a different design on a production and you go, "No, that's wrong." But in fact, for somebody who's never seen the original production it's quite acceptable. In many cases the lighter designs of the Danish production [of *Manon*] bring out different things in the choreography. But it's swings and round-abouts. I used to love the feeling of dirt about the Georgiadis designs in *Manon* and the nasty dirty feel of the period, and the Danish [design] is…very Danish, very clean.

I was coming in today and thinking, 'Why on earth am I coming in to talk about ballet?' Because in this kind of [world] climate, that's the last thing that one should be talking about. But…How can one put it succinctly? I think the classics bring a breath of fresh air. I can watch *Swan Lake*…I *have* watched *Swan Lake* so many times, and you come to that fourth act and you really feel wonderful, listening to it and watching it, I'm taken away by it. *Sleeping Beauty*'s got some marvelous moments in it, and there's a refreshing quality about it for the public. It's like *Nutcracker*. The children love *Nutcracker*—the parents seem to hate it, but the children love it. Essentially one's got to say it's the music, it's sensational. There's got to be a logical reason why we love these things, but why...? Why does one like listening to music? Why does one like looking at art? Ballet's like seeing a wonderful painting, except it's live performance.

It's changing, oh my goodness, it's changed. I remember when I did my first *Sylphides* they tried to make me wear one of those wigs. There was a lovely dancer called Alexander Bennett, and he'd been doing *Sylphides* at the Royal Ballet touring company and he thought it was absolutely dreadful that I should not put the wig on for my rehearsal. Which was probably right, but somehow I did get away with it. I said to John Field, "I don't want to wear the wig," because I think I'd seen Rudolf and he hadn't worn the wig. So I was allowed not to wear the wig, but that's the way things move on.

Fundamentally, of course, ballet's not changing, because of the work that goes into producing things on the stage. You can't do it in any other way. You can't take a pill and go, "We won't do class, we won't rehearse, there we are." It's the commitment and preparation to producing a performance that won't change, and I think all of the dancers are committed. They all go out clubbing and things like that, which we used to do in our day, but the next morning we'd be there [in class], doing our bit.

I couldn't have wished to have been involved in anything more fulfilling than ballet. Certainly the performing side of things was lovely, but I got just as much out of being a ballet master and teaching. Looking back to the early days...I'm now being asked to talk about things that I didn't think I'd ever be asked to talk about, not only by you, so one is casting one's mind back constantly. And I must say the first years of my career, from the age of 16 to sort of 21, were such fun, before one had a lot of responsibility and pressure at the opera house. I suppose there was a lot of responsibility in the performances one was giving, but somehow it was such terrible fun, we were so naughty. And I think about the places we went, Baalbek...oh, we used to do yearly tours of the continent, Spain... we schlepped around everywhere. The dancers are missing that fun now. This company tours, but in a very different way. Their provincial tours at the most are six weeks. We used to do two 14-week provincial tours each year plus a season at the opera house plus an overseas tour. You got a lot of experience in a year, which held one in good stead.

I think I was a successful dancer and I think I was a good ballet master, but you can't do it by yourself. And I've always had the support of Freda, she somehow kept my feet quite firmly on the ground, which was I think a benefit to the way I performed. And the other influence of course is the choreographers, Tudor, Ashton, MacMillan, people that created ballets for you are so important. Oh, I loved Tudor, he was my mentor. I thought, 'He's so wise,' and he was clever, he used to be able to get inside you. I just wish I'd been ten years older when I worked with him, because I think I could have got more out of him. Well, he made me start thinking. You get on the treadmill and…I wanted to know about him and he wouldn't let me know anything—with Tudor you're always so far away.

We did a ballet called *Knight Errant*; he did it a few months after *Shadowplay*, it was fantastic. But it was a difficult time inasmuch as I had the beginnings of a really bad injury that kept me off dancing for a year. So I was trying to perform and create and worry about this injury, which in fact stopped me from doing the first night of the ballet, which was such a disappointment. But still, what happened during the process of working is that we became really good friends and really soulmates, if you could ever become a soulmate of Tudor's.

We've been trying to bring it alive again recently, but it wasn't taped or notated and it was a wonderful piece. It was *Liaisons Dangereuses*, one act set around one of the letters—he didn't tell us any of this—and it was to Strauss, *Bourgeois Gentilhomme* and *Ariadne* [*auf Naxos*]. The more I think about it, the more I think, 'Oh god, that was quite amazing.' But it's in the dim distant past, 40 years ago, but *he's* not, that's the thing. One can see that back and those eyes and that bald head and that humor.

Now I don't think of what's coming. I'm happy to assist and help out whenever invited. But I think I owe it to my family and Freda to have a little bit of…what's it called?…not even down time, not even free time, *quality* time and doing things I like to do, which is not a lot. I've decided that had I not been a dancer I'd have been a really lazy person. It's so nice not actually working to a schedule, because apart from school, if you actually contemplate, when you join a company you've got 10:30 class and then every hour is spoken for until you retire. The same with a ballet master really, except you do a little bit more than the dancers.

London
November 2008

Merrill Ashley

Merrill Ashley (b. St. Paul, Minnesota, 1950) began to study ballet at the age of seven in Vermont. In 1963, after her second summer at the School of American Ballet, she moved to New York to continue her training at the School while attending the Professional Children's School. She joined New York City Ballet in 1967 and progressed to the rank of soloist in 1974 and of principal three years later. Acclaimed for her dazzling technique and streamlined attack in such ballets as *Square Dance* and *Theme and Variations*, she embraced a diverse repertory of dramatic and lyrical works as well, and created leading roles in Balanchine's *Ballo della Regina* (1978) and *Ballade* (1980) and in Peter Martins' *Barber Violin Concerto* (1988) and *Fearful Symmetries* (1990). Exploring new territory, she led a small touring company during the summers of 1981 and 1982, and danced *Sleeping Beauty* and *Paquita* as a guest artist with Sadler's Wells Royal Ballet in London in 1987. Since retiring in 1997, she has appeared in character roles with New York City Ballet, the Royal Danish Ballet and Boston Ballet.

§§§

One of Balanchine's most devoted disciples, Ashley has staged his ballets internationally since 1990 on behalf of the George Balanchine Trust and lectured regularly about his work for the George Balanchine Foundation. She is the co-author and co-artistic director of an educational video series, "The Balanchine Essays," which documents the meticulously defined principles she has also taught to advanced students at the School of American Ballet and in professional masterclasses all over the world. Having returned to New York City Ballet as a Teaching

Associate from 1998 to 2008, she served as a guest teacher there from 2009 to 2012. The 30-year period between our conversations exactly duplicates the length of her performing life with that company.

§§§

I always wanted my dancing to be versatile, I always wanted to be elegant. I wanted to be technically secure, correct from a technical point of view. I wanted to be musical. I had a kind of all-American look, and my spirit is very energetic and joyful. So while I did lyrical roles and I think I could do them well, I was noted for my speed, my clarity, my energy...those things were important. But being versatile was really important to me. I didn't want to be typecast...although in the end I sort of was typecast, as the classical virtuoso.

I was always trying to take really good care of my body, and yet my body was constantly injured, and that was hard. Just when I'd start to feel I was maybe about to acquire something new, an injury would come. On the other hand, even though it was hard to believe in the midst of *not* dancing, I found that when I came back from a bad injury I was a better dancer artistically in ways I could not have imagined. The anguish, the pain I went through, the uncertainty, somehow I could add all that to different roles. The joy of being back onstage I could bring to other roles. There were little technical problems that I knew I always had, and as I came back from square one yet again, I tried to eliminate those problems, when the habits weren't so ingrained anymore. I think I learned better ways to take care of my body...I learned a different way of working. I used my brain more; rather than repeating a step that wasn't working over and over again, I really tried to figure out what was wrong, take it apart so I didn't bash my body so much. And through analyzing things like that, you start seeing what your tendencies are and you start watching other people. How do they cope with the situation that's causing you so much trouble? What do they do? Is it technique, is it timing—what is it? You really have an opportunity to reexamine a lot and learn a lot.

I didn't choose to retire—it was the injuries without a doubt. And because I love what Balanchine taught me, I feel I want to pass that on, not only want to but I have a responsibility to, and it's not a burden. Actually, it is in certain ways, because there's so much to pass on and so many people to pass it on to and it's impossible to pass it on enough. But it's something I love deeply and if I can illuminate that for other people, make them understand the benefits of what he taught, technically and visually, and help his ballets survive in a way that was reminiscent of what he wanted when he choreographed them, that is very gratifying and satisfying.

When I retired, the dilemma was, Do I teach at the School [of American Ballet], do I work for the company, do I work for another company? When do I have hip surgery? I'd spent a long time avoiding it—should I give in and do it right away or should I keep fighting? That was a biggy. I spoke to Peter [Martins, Ballet Master in Chief of New York City Ballet] first, and his first idea was for me to teach at the School, and I said, "I really think I have more to offer the company." I like to teach, but teaching is a lot of giving in one way, and I said, "I also think I have [other] things to give, and it provides more variety if I have teaching and coaching." I felt I could be valuable in that regard; there were a lot of young dancers, and he was going to need a lot of help to develop them.

What I do now is teach company class, usually twice a week, occasionally three times a week. And then I coach Balanchine ballets, the ones I'm assigned—it's not a free-for-all—primarily the ones I danced. Basically I'm coaching the principals; sometimes, like *Raymonda* [*Variations*], I do the soloists. If Sean [Lavery] and I are in a rehearsal together, it's not that I can't say something about the men and he can't say something about the women, but I think our focus goes to our own gender. And the one ballet I stage completely is *Ballo* [*della Regina*].

When I first started teaching I could still dance. My plan was to keep in toe shoes and kind of do barre and some other steps that were comfortable. I couldn't lift my legs, but I could still move, I could still jump, I could still turn. So I thought, 'This will help me make the transition, because I can still get into a step, so I'll be able to think what to say in terms of "Feel this" or "Feel that," connecting verbally with the physical.' And I'd still be facile enough physically that I could show it, not full out maybe, or if I tried to imitate them I could feel what wasn't right.

Soon enough, in about two weeks, I fell and sprained my ankle really badly—I ripped tendons—walking into the theatre. Because of the way I walked due to my hip problem, I hit the outside of my foot instead of the whole heel, and the sprain just ruined my ankle. And that was the end of…class, taking class, being in pointe shoes, that was the end. Then about every six months the same thing happened, I fell and sprained my ankle because of the way I was walking. I was still teaching, but with a sprained ankle I really couldn't show anything or feel anything. And I found that hard because I'm not good at making up steps. I'm much better if I can get up and move around, but to do it in my head? That's not very easy for me, and suddenly that's the only thing I had. It was kind of an abrupt change from dancer to teacher, a teacher that couldn't move too well.

I also felt that the things I had given myself to warm up were very much related to what Mr. B [Balanchine] taught. Before every performance, I did 16 tendus front, side and back. That's how I got warm. Well, from every other dancer's point of view, that was very extreme. If I give 16 tendus front, side and back in class now, they're not likely to come back tomorrow. So in the beginning my classes were much too difficult for people. They expected a warm-up, and I was not giving them a warm-up. I was trying to warm them up, but I was trying to *teach* them something, and to build speed and build stamina and be very refined and very aware, trying to include all his habits, all those things that he did in class. I was trying to be a little more considerate physically, to get them warm before they did it, but I was trying to incorporate those principles. And I could sense resistance, big time. Little by little the classes started to get smaller, and I thought, 'OK, you can either keep going this way or you can change. Because how can you help people if they're not in class? You either have to make it more palatable or you're not going to have anybody to teach.' So I changed. It rubs me the wrong way, but I can still work on a lot of things. My class reputation is that it's not a warm-up. It's hard.

Inevitably…When you teach, your personality is going to come out. The kinds of steps that pop into your mind are related, some-what, to what you like to do or have a point that is important to you, be it clarity or speed or control or placement or épaulement, whatever it is. But I also remember Balanchine always saying, "You have to look at them and give them what they need." So I try and do that, I try and see what they need.

Now I see less épaulement, less use of the head and arms, less precision, smaller steps—we used to really step out, now the size of the step they take is what's comfortable. I work on those things all the time, along with placement of the feet, how we put our feet down, and I often feel…They hear me harping on it, but they don't understand the importance of it. They don't see it and they don't care, or they don't want to make the effort. We're going back to quantity instead of quality in ballet, and yet there's more talent than ever before. The young dancers that come in the company...Just take pirouettes as an example. When I joined, I couldn't do a double pirouette regularly. Now they're all doing triple pirouettes and four and five—it's normal. I never could and I didn't even try, because Balanchine just wanted two clear turns, no more. Today most people have extremely high extensions. But they're not doing a lot of other things. It's not that somebody at the School hasn't asked for it, but somehow it hasn't become ingrained.

The other thing that's changed at the School is that it never used to be informal. With the Russians there was a discipline and a respect and a formality. You didn't go talk to Tumey [Antonina Tumkovsky] and [Hélène] Dudin and talk about your toe shoes and this problem and that problem. They were teachers; you weren't to burden them with those things. They told you what to do, you tried to do it in class and you left, and they went somewhere else. I think now the teachers often become friends with the students. Our teachers weren't our friends. They were respected icons, up there and over there, and there was a distance. And the discipline they insisted on is not there now.

And the whole attitude toward one's career is different. When I was in the company the career was everything. You weren't worrying about school, about boyfriends, about your social life, about what you were going to wear...You were worried about looking beautiful in class, pleasing Mr. Balanchine and learning how to dance beautifully. That's what your life was. You walked into that theatre, it was...not a religion but that theatre was a revered place, and you behaved well in it and it was the most important place in your life. That is not the case now. Everybody has a boyfriend, everybody's going to school. In my opinion, you have to focus on your career first—now they get in the company and they think they're finished dancers. That's the way they act, like, 'OK, if my career doesn't work out...' But then they don't develop as dancers, and suddenly they're wondering why their career isn't going anywhere or not going fast enough.

The repertoire still holds dancers there. To be able to do all those Balanchine and Robbins ballets, that's a big draw. And dancing them, especially the Balanchine ballets, defines the company and keeps the technique at a certain level and a certain style. It forces you technically to acquire certain skills. There are certain things that are taught at the School that become second nature to New York City Ballet dancers, like spotting front on the diagonal, bringing your arms close to your body at the appropriate moments...It's not always taught *when* that's appropriate, but they've experienced it. Whereas other dancers outside have never experienced it, and spotting front, arms close to the body, speed, are very hard if you haven't been brought up with it. When you stage a ballet somewhere else, you spend all your time trying to get those things from them because they have no idea about them.

My teaching has to be different everywhere I go, and the adjustment depends first of all on how much I'm going to teach. When I go somewhere I haven't taught before, I end up talking so much in class that I actually announce it *before*. I say, "The first two classes, I'm going to be talking a lot, because the principles that I'm going to ask you for are complicated and I want you to understand the reason I'm asking for them. It's not just an arbitrary command, 'Put your foot here.' There's a reason for it, and for the Balanchine ballets you're going to be doing, it will be necessary, and we have to practice it." I really wish I didn't have to talk a lot, but I cannot find a way around it, because otherwise they think, 'I've never had to do a tendu like this before. Why? What difference does it make?'

Certainly when I got to Hong Kong, very few of the dancers had ever had any exposure to Balanchine's ballets or the style or the technique. I've been there twice; I was staging *Tchaikovsky Pas de Deux* and helping rehearse *Theme and Variations*, and god knows, Balanchine technique is needed in both of those. I mean, you can't *do* them any other way. It's so hard to distill it down, not talk too much, get them warm, make them understand, fit it in an hour and 15 minutes, find a way to make it palatable...And I didn't want to turn them off. I really felt some people were listening, others seemed to have earplugs in their ears, I didn't know if they were getting it. Also there's a language problem: did they even understand the words I was saying? Then one day this girl came up to me and said, "I don't understand what you mean here. Can you explain it more?" Then she asked me about something else—and this was a girl I thought was not interested at all—and I thought, 'My god, I've reached people more than I think.' So you never can be sure who you're reaching.

I feel I make more headway when I'm coaching, because suddenly it's a step that they're going to have to do in front of 3,000 people, not just for the teachers, and it matters. In Cuba the dancers were like vacuum cleaners, they sucked in whatever I offered. First of all, the ballet was a revelation to them—I staged *Ballo* there [for the National Ballet of Cuba]. Now, that is really different from what they've been doing. Lorena Feijoo got it. I really had to work with her, but she was so technically proficient and so refined already and malleable enough that stylistically she could change. Some of the others couldn't, but they liked the ballet. They've been so sheltered and so cocooned, it was like being in a smoke-filled room and suddenly it clears and you have this rush of mountain air. Wow, did they want it!

The bigger and more established the company, the more resistance you can encounter. Paris doesn't want it. Paris was a nightmare for me. I wasn't staging a ballet, it was a masterclass and I taught there [at the Paris Opéra Ballet] for two weeks. Violette [Verdy] recommended me, so I went, and the first class was packed, the second class was less packed, by the end of the week I had four people—it was really a jolt. Then, I don't know, these four people were devoted. It was clear they really wanted to be there, they kept coming, so I really gave them everything I had. Then little by little a few more people started coming, and by the time I left…it wasn't packed but it was respectable.

Then in 2004, there was a kind of Balanchine symposium, and I went and gave one masterclass to the Kirov. Talk about being nervous! Some people tried, some people gave up. Toward the end of the class I gave a step from *Square Dance*—jeté battu, ballonné battu, glissade, jeté battu, ballonné battu—at the tempo the corps de ballet does it. The pianist wouldn't even *play* it as fast as I asked, and [Diana] Vishneva was the only one who really attempted it, she went to the end of the step. Everybody else, they'd start and then go, 'I can't. Ridiculous.' There I was, doing it, two artificial hips and ankles that can't jump, and yet they can't. It is an attitude. I mean, if you never practice moving your legs that way…It *is* a technique, but it's an attitude of being willing to try and willing to go through the humiliation of not being able to do it.

You know, Balanchine kept us humble in class. He was always giving us steps that we couldn't do. He was always saying, "No, it's not good enough." Always. From the lowest corps member to

Suzanne [Farrell], if you count her as the top, he was striving to get more out of us, to keep us from becoming arrogant, keep us always learning and willing to try, all the time. Then you can accept corrections, you can accept that you don't know how to do something. If you keep that attitude of constantly trying to improve, constantly trying to refine what you do, admitting that you have flaws, that you need to work on things, that you have weaknesses, then when you're in a ballet that's a struggle for you, it's OK, you can take it on.

But often the dancers cannot tolerate that—dancers anywhere, even in New York City Ballet. They're offended by the criticism or by the awareness that they're not versatile enough or that they might have difficulty changing, and instead of being open they just shut down. They get defensive, because they sense that they're rigid in their approach, and they're not humble enough to admit they have a problem and to listen to what you have to say. But Balanchine was training us to work like that. Once I heard him say to Suzanne, his favorite, "Don't run like a truck driver." That's humiliating. But she accepted the criticism and changed the way she ran.

When I went to London in '87...I did *Sleeping Beauty* partly because it was offered to me and partly because Balanchine was gone and that stimulation, that learning process from him, had ended. It was a period in New York City Ballet when, even though I should have been dancing a lot, I wasn't dancing a lot. I was kind of under-employed, and I was sort of in my prime and I wanted to dance. And...I was established. Nobody was really looking out for me anymore, trying to challenge me, which Balanchine always did. He was always there, making us neater, tidier, more proficient, and when he choreographed he gave me the most impossible steps. He was definitely challenging me, but I liked the challenge, and certainly trying to change styles...My approach to *Sleeping Beauty* was...I wanted to remain true to my Balanchinian roots and yet make certain modifications in that style, to be a little more contained in my port de bras, a little... less abandoned, much more on balance, not going through one's balance. And that was very hard.

I think technically I was prepared for it but not mentally, in a funny way. Balanchine never talked about acting or mood or how to develop a character in a ballet. John [Meehan] helped me a lot, and Violette helped me too, and a ballet master in London, Desmond Kelly. We just kept polishing for those performances.

You know, Balanchine helped me a lot in many roles, but it wasn't that kind of daily coaching, on the same thing, over and over and over again. It was, Here's the rehearsal, we'd go through it, this is what I have to say to you and now you're on your own to figure out how to do what I'm asking you to do. Whereas with *Sleeping Beauty* I had somebody coaching me every day, trying to solve the trouble spots and help me tie it all together. That was new, and that was good.

So now, when suddenly I'm having to coach full-length *Swan Lake*, which I never danced, and *Sleeping Beauty*, which I did do, I have sympathy for the difficulties these dancers are facing. They're young, they're not even experienced. Sara Mearns had never done a solo in the company before she did Swan Queen. These are *young* people, with nothing to back them up, not even technique sometimes. So Sean and I were having to take the principals from stage zero to creating a character, finding the technique, building the stamina, relating to your partner, dealing with the pressure, all of it.

My coaching depends on the season. You only work on the ballets that you're assigned. So this season, I have second movement Bizet [*Symphony in C*] and fourth movement *Brahms* [*Brahms-Schoenberg Quartet*], because this season is all Robbins. Some seasons it's a lot of Balanchine, certainly the Balanchine Centennial I had a lot to do. So every season is different. Sean and I often rehearse ballets together, *Theme* [*and Variations*] we do together, *Piano Concerto* [*No. 2*], *Brahms*, Bizet, a lot of ballets like that. So if one of us has an opportunity to do freelance work and the other can stay and rehearse the ballet, that's OK. But you can't abandon the ballet. If *Ballo* goes [on] in New York and I want to go do *Ballo* in Pennsylvania, too bad. Or I'd have to find a way to rehearse it here first, make sure it's ready, and then be away and come back for the first performance.

The hardest part is to try and find the soul...you know, a spirit behind it. It's not just a bunch of steps, and if you watched Balanchine move, you could see it, so you have to try and convey that. But the problem is that when they're not used to training their eyes to see slight refinement in movement, they can't see the difference. Maybe they see the difference but they can't analyze it, they can't see that this croisé is different from that croisé. If I do one of each, yes, there's a difference, but what's the difference? And why does it matter? They don't use the whole body to do a movement.

It's like they have appendages stuck on and they use them, but the rest of the body doesn't participate.

Steps create effects. Steps are meant to be beautiful or impressive or create a reaction. He used to say, "Patty McBride can turn like the wind." You could give her any combination with a turn and she could just do it. You get to somebody else who's not as natural a turner, and they're going to struggle. So what's the point of making that dancer do turns that don't look good? Hopefully the dancer tries to learn how to do the step. But if after quite a bit of work they're still not comfortable and it looks awkward or insecure, why force them to do a step that's not a signature step in a ballet? In *Ballo* you can't change pirouette to plié, pirouette to plié, it's a signature step. But the preparation into that can be changed, and certain things I changed myself in *Ballo* as the years went on. So I know from dancing it where the most awkward moments are, and I know what the key is to get into that particular turn. So if I can find a preparation that will help the dancer make the signature step work, as opposed to not work with the original preparation, to me it's a no-brainer. A lot of times the steps do change, sometimes not on purpose. Nobody notices or people notice but they can't say anything. Then there's a videotape of that performance, and then somebody wants to go stage a ballet and they look at that videotape and that mistake is carried forward.

The dancers rely on video a lot, more and more. Sometimes it's an emergency: somebody's out, we're going to rehearse this tomorrow, here's a tape. But that's not the standard procedure. We have so many ballets to do and so much repertoire to rehearse and often not enough time to rehearse it that often what happens…The dancers are taught first, not always but usually. They have a rehearsal, they learn some steps, it's a quick learning process, and there's not time to go back and make sure they know it. So they study the videotapes to review it and then they see, "Oh, that step's different. On the tape I watched it's a different step, and what should I do?" That leaves all of us confused. Finally it's the ballet master or mistress that has to make a decision.

Sometimes you realize you made a mistake and you go back and try and fix it the next season. "But we didn't do that last season." "Well, we're going to do it that way this season." Then the next season comes along and some people were out and they come back and they do it the old way. So the ballets are becoming less focused. There's very little time spent on how the ballets should look, the mood of the ballet. It's about what are the patterns, just learn the steps and do it, be in the right place at the right time on the proper foot. The musicality isn't focused on, lots of things aren't focused on, and the ballets look...unfocused. It's the best word I can think of. Some of those moments that were iconic moments are now just steps—they are correct, but it just doesn't look like anything.

But the dancers are so rarely given an opportunity to really work on a ballet for weeks on end. Most of the time the casting's done pretty much at the last minute. If it's a new role, they have maybe a week to learn it and work on it, then they're onstage, and then they're on to the next thing. They have two performances and then maybe they don't do it for a year. Especially with the block programing we're doing now, it's even harder to give dancers an opportunity to do many performances of a ballet. Let's say last season Ashley Bouder did all the *Piano Concertos*—not that she did, but let's just say. Then the next season it's scheduled with a new ballet that she's in. So somebody else is going to do all the *Piano Concertos* because she can't do both ballets, and that program stays the same—it's always going to have *Piano Concerto* without her and new ballet with her. Whereas in the past, with the mixed programs, she's in the new ballet the night of the première, and somebody else is in *Piano Concerto*. But the next night, the new ballet doesn't go when *Piano Concerto* goes, so she gets to do her *Piano Concerto*. So the opportunity was there to juggle the casting more. Now you're forced into certain casting whether you like it or you don't like it.

The skill that the dancers are cultivating is the skill of learning a ballet quickly and having enough facility to get the steps done. That's what they're working on. They are not working on refinement or understanding what the spirit of the ballet is. They are not working on the music. It's not uppermost in their mind unless they have somebody taking the rehearsal that insists on it. But for the corps de ballet, they don't get that at all. They have to figure it out themselves.

Yes, I did too, but I was figuring it out from a much more refined point of view, with ultra-refinement being noticed and cared about and scrutinized and insisted upon, and to hell with the rehearsal schedule. Balanchine would take...I remember...We were doing *Square Dance*, and there's a step where the boys have a very funny preparation, kind of a wide, turned-in preparation, double pirouette, fourth, double pirouette, fourth. Half an hour he spent trying to get those boys to do that step the way he wanted. Half an hour. We had a performance that night, the guys' thighs were burning, dying, the rest of the ballet still had to be rehearsed, I was standing around, the rest of the program had to be rehearsed—he didn't care. It was important to him and he was going to kill himself to get what he wanted. And that made it clear to you that It Was Important. It's not just somebody saying, "Fourth...oh, it doesn't matter so much. It's uncomfortable. We don't practice that in class. I'm going to do it my way." No. He cared, he wanted it, and damned if you weren't going to try and do it.

But also, when you're trying to do something like [choreography by Mauro] Bigonzetti or [Jorma] Elo—these days, all companies have to do that—kind of wiggly, wobbly...I don't know what to call it, but it's not ballet technique the way I think of ballet technique, and I think it makes dancing much harder. I don't know how to say this...It's less urgent to have good ballet technique, because often the ballets don't require ballet technique. Like last season, Tess [Reichlen] was doing *Piano Concerto* for the first time, and I had six weeks to rehearse her. It was unheard of that we had that much time, but she needed it and she came a long way in it. But at the same time she was rehearsing some new ballet, it was Bigonzetti, so she'd come from a rehearsal of the new ballet into *Piano Concerto*. I felt terrible for her, because to let your body go to do Bigonzetti and then to have to pull it together for the most refined, technically challenging ballet that had everything that she needs to work on, grandeur and aura and presence and a certain kind of technique, to try and clean it up and get it right and get the épaulement...I thought, 'You poor girl. It's hard enough to do this. You should be doing this from 12:00 to 1:00 and then go do your Bigonzetti.' But the schedule doesn't work that way.

One of the biggest differences from when I was in the company...Aside from rehearsing with whoever taught me the ballet, which was usually another dancer, or rehearsing with Balanchine after I'd kind of learned it, every other rehearsal was by myself. I didn't have a coach there watching me—I did it all myself, we all did it all ourselves. We'd have request rehearsals. You'd request, "I want to rehearse with my partner on *Donizetti* [*Variations*]," and you'd have a room and a pianist for an hour but nobody sitting there telling you, "This is good" or "Change your angle... Your foot's not pointed there," nobody. There were times when Balanchine spent a lot of time with you, maybe two or three rehearsals. But then I was on my own again to take whatever he had said and incorporate it.

Now there's a ballet mistress there. Every cast gets a full stage rehearsal—we never had that. The dancers are allowed to ask for request rehearsals, but the ballet masters are responsible for making sure that we've looked at what they're going to do. So I think they don't know how to think for themselves anymore, even very intelligent people. Sofiane [Sylve] is not inexperienced, she's not dumb, she's very technically secure, and she said to me, "I cannot rehearse in a room alone. I can't. I *must* have somebody there." I don't know why. Maybe she's just never tried to do it by herself.

The thing that bugs me about dancers these days...Sean and I take the young, talented dancers and rehearse, let's say, Sugar Plum pas de deux. Sometimes we teach it to two or three couples at a time and then we rehearse them separately, and we really spend weeks trying to teach them some of the basic things, place your foot, give your hand beautifully, turn out, use your plié, pull up in your hip, partnering, we really break it down for them. Then comes the next ballet, which has many of the same elements, and you have to break it down for them again. They cannot find a way to take what they learn in one ballet and apply it to something else. I've taken dancers aside and said, "Look, we worked on it, and you made all this progress. It's not just for *Nutcracker*. You have to do that in every ballet: you have to place your feet, you have to turn out, you have to hold yourself, you have to use your elbows, your wrists, your head. You have to think about it and carry it over." And they do it for a little while or for that season and then...

One principal dancer, she's one of the younger ones, we worked on *Nutcracker*, I worked on her arms so hard, and they improved. And when we came back to *Nutcracker* the next year, it was as if we had never done anything, not the feet, not the arms, not the head, not the presentation—she looked like she had just come out of the School. I was just appalled and I said, "You know, we've been doing this for three years, and every year we start at the same place. You should be progressing. There are many other things to talk about, but I can't get there because we're starting over again every time. If you want to grow, you have to take responsibility for yourself and not only maintain what we give you in Ballet A but apply it to Ballet B, C, D, E and F. You have to."

They used to record every performance, but they don't anymore. Now they do the first time a ballet goes in a season and [when] there's a new cast, a debut. You can learn a lot from video. You can learn what not to do, you can see variations from one performance to the next, you can get ideas. Sometimes you can solve some partnering things, you really do find some technical clues. And to be able to go and watch your own performance... It's not a perfect reflection of what was done, but as a teaching tool for yourself...

I've actually offered...I said to three or four different people, "Let's take the video of your performance last night, and I'll go through it with you, and I'll tell you what I thought was good and where I think you need improvement." No one has taken me up on it, which I find odd. I mean, if I had had a principal dancer come to me and say, "I'll go over a performance with you," and we watched it together...what a valuable experience. As a coach I could say, "See, you really did what we worked on, that was great," or "You see that bad line? That's what I haven't been able to fix." Nobody wants to do that, and I think that would be a really profitable, valuable use of videotape.

The idea for the Balanchine Essays came about right after Balanchine died, and we thought, 'These details are going to get lost.' A dancer knows from doing...You learn a ballet and you do the ballet and you know the ballet. Three or four years go by, and you go back to it, and inevitably little things...What was the step there? What's the musicality here? and What arm did I use? Or you wait ten years, and it's that much vaguer. Well, we knew the same thing was going to happen with Balanchine technique. And while it was as fresh as it could be in our minds, we wanted to record everything we could think of about it and have it there as a record. That was the original conception.

It was for anybody who was interested—dancers, choreographers, dance historians—because there are so many misconceptions about Balanchine technique, and that's really irritating. So we wanted to dispel the myth of the incorrectness, we wanted to record as much detail as we could, and we wanted to show examples of it in the classroom and in his ballets. Dance is dance, and you can't just write about it or talk about it or take still pictures of it—you have to move.

It took us a while to find the right format. I think we did maybe two different approaches before we hit on the one that we used. Of course, time went by as we did all that, but as I remember it, Suki [Schorer] and I got together before we started filming and tried to go over all the points that we wanted to talk about. So we had made notes, we had that outline, and when we found the formula, with me as the expert demonstrating, students behind me doing the same steps and Suki doing the talking, we started doing the filming. Suki and I agreed on everything—she's a generation earlier than me—except I remember changing rond de jambe à terre. At one point he wanted an accent like this, from second to tendu back with the accent to the back, and then later he changed it, there's no accent, it's a circle and there's no beginning and no end. Suki said "It used to be this," and I said, "Yes, but for my whole time in the company, from 1967 on, it was a circle with no accent."

He'd change a step in a ballet, but the actual technique of what he asked for, how the hands moved, how the head moved, where the tilt was…we practiced that. In class we'd do, Tilt your head, Go back to straight, Tilt your head, Back to straight, Tilt your head, Back to straight. There was a very specific angle you were supposed to put your head at, it's not just, Turn to the side. And croisé is this, and écarté is this, and the fingers and where your elbows are and how much your arms move—all that never changed.

I know the public has changed. I don't really know who the audience is now, but to me, they go with a much more superficial expectation. What I think of as the old City Ballet audience are people that want to see a ballet 20 times because it's so interesting and there's so much to see and it's different every time, and they want to see a million casts—they get into it. The people nowadays don't want to see a ballet twice; that's why our subscription is the way it is. Before the fixed programs, they would buy two subscriptions, say for every Tuesday night, and Peter got complaints: "I don't want to see, within my two subscriptions, a repeat of one ballet." So it's more like it's a superficial entertainment, let's just have a little of this, a little of that, a little of something else, and let's not delve into this too deeply. And it's much more like a social status symbol: I go to the ballet every week. But do they truly care about it? I don't think so.

I don't take that into account. To me, quality dancing will stir an audience. Whether they know why they're being affected or not, they are and they respond. When it's just average or mediocre...they almost don't know sometimes that it's not good. But that's not my concern. My concern is to try to create quality and hope that the quality has an effect on audience members that makes them want to come back again. But you have to make people want to watch you. I mean, writers write, and if it's not good, you start the book and you put it down, you don't want to bother with it. Quality in anything is appealing to people, it hooks them.

And I think arts in general are needed. If people's lives are too devoid of whatever that spiritual thing is that we get from art, somehow they realize that something's missing. But whether ballet is going to be what gives them that feeling, I don't know. The works that stir me are the ones that have the most clear connection to traditional ballet, that are not just wiggly movement, turned in and ugly with no connection to the music that's obvious to me. Going to New York City Ballet and seeing the programs that seem to rouse the audience the most, Balanchine's still up there as the best. The all-Balanchine programs are much more popular, oh yeah, it's very clear. And it seems that after a Balanchine ballet people are a little more animated when they get up out of their seats. Somehow they realize that something happened, and it wasn't just ho-hum.

And more and more companies around the world are turning to Balanchine...It's like they use Balanchine ballets as an anchor to a program and a lure to the audience members to come in: 'Well, if you like new things, then you're curious and you're going to come and see the new ballet. And you're going to have something meaty, your main course is the Balanchine ballet.' Even when people are not familiar with it, there's a modicum of safety there. Even though it's a novelty, you program it with the knowledge that it is quality, it's solid, and you're going to get something valuable from it. There can be something kind of obviously superficial and nice about it, and then if you have the eyes to see—and it's danced well enough—you see an inner aspect too that hits you at a deeper level.

There are very few of us left. We're the last generation that worked with him. Those of us that are in a position to pass on our knowledge have a responsibility to do it and we have to do it well, because there are a lot of misconceptions everywhere. In some places Balanchine's a dirty word, and that just kills me, it's like a dagger in my heart. So anything that I can do to clarify what he did give and to enlighten dancers...Dancing his way enhances one's pleasure in dancing—I don't know how else to say it. It happens so often when I'm rehearsing a Balanchine ballet, especially outside the company when they've never tried some of these things before...There's some step they're struggling with, and finally I convince them to try the technique or they are able to incorporate what I've said, and suddenly they're not afraid of the step anymore, suddenly it's fun to dance and they see it work and they see me respond and everybody else in the room responds. Those moments are so thrilling, to see them see the light and see that there's a physical logic to it.

But I can't force them. It's like Mr. B said. He was so frustrated in class one day. He said, "You know, I can decide on the menu, I can go out and buy the food for you, I can clean it, I can cut it up, I can cook it, I can even chew it for you, but I can't swallow it for you. You have to swallow it." If those dancers are not interested in swallowing what I can give them, I can't force it. I will turn my attention to somebody who's interested in what I have to say, and they'll benefit from it, and the others will lose out. It's up to them.

So my approach now, at least at New York City Ballet, is to focus on the young people that join the company. Joining the company is an overwhelming experience. First of all, you're usually one of the better ones in the School, you've been given all the lead roles in the [annual] Workshop [performance], you think you're pretty good. Then you get in the company, you're overwhelmed, you're trying to learn everything, you don't get the personal attention anymore, and maybe because you think you're pretty good, you don't really work, you relax. My feeling is that it's my responsibility to stay on top of those people while they're still in the learning frame of mind—they were just in the School, so they're accustomed to hearing corrections—and try and keep their brain open to the idea that there's still a lot to learn, and help them before they get jaded. And then, in addition to that, help the people that seem open to what I have to say, and hope that other people will see that they become more interesting to watch.

It's like Tess. I never felt Tess paid attention to what I said in class, it was like an aggravation for her. Maybe she was mad at herself, I don't know, but that was the impression I had, and she didn't take my class very much, so I figured I wasn't hitting home with her. Then we got to *Piano Concerto* and she really struggled, and three or four times in the first rehearsal she said, "They make this look so easy—this is hard!" And she kept struggling and she couldn't do it and she couldn't do it and she couldn't do it. And one day...We'd worked for about a month on one thing, sauté, chassé, and I said, "You have to get your feet together in chassé. You'll never get into the next step, and it doesn't look good. Get your feet together." Finally she did it, and everything was easier. And she looked at me, huffing and puffing, and she said, "You're just like my mother. You're always right." But you know, finally, finally, the ballet humbled her. She couldn't do it without help, and I gave her the tools.

New York
April 2008

Nina Ananiashvili

Nina Ananiashvili (b. Tbilisi, Republic of Georgia, 1964) began her ballet training at the Georgian State Choreographic School in Tbilisi in 1973, the year she was named Georgia's junior ice-skating champion. She entered the Moscow Choreographic Institute at thirteen and was still a student when she claimed gold medals in the 1980 Varna International Competition and in the junior division of the 1981 Moscow International Competition. Having joined the Bolshoi Ballet in 1981, she made her debut in *Swan Lake* a year later, before leaving the corps de ballet. Coached by Raisa Struchkova and Marina Semyonova, in 1985 she was awarded principal status and ever greater access to the classical repertory, from *Giselle* to *Don Quixote*. In 1986 she and Andris Liepa were the first Soviet participants in the international competition in Jackson, Mississippi, and the first competitors ever to win its Grand Prix. Two years later, they became the first Soviet dancers to guest with New York City Ballet. Probably the busiest dancer of her generation, Ananiashvili retained her position with the Bolshoi while making regular appearances with American Ballet Theatre (1993–2009) and fulfilling guest engagements all over the world, partnered by Liepa, Alexei Fadeyechev and each company's resident danseurs. Between those obligations, she established concert groups in 1992 and 2000, with which she toured internationally. She continues to appear regularly with the State Ballet of Georgia, which she has directed since 2004.

§§§

The second edition of *Striking a Balance* contains several interviews, Ananiashvili's among them, that did not appear in the original edition published ten years earlier. The youngest artist in the book in 1992, Ananiashvili is now the only one still performing, so her perspectives as dancer and director overlap constantly. We spoke in Edinburgh, where the State Ballet of Georgia had arrived for its debut at the Edinburgh International Festival just as Georgia and Russia went to war.

§§§

You know, my life is totally changed after the '90s, because I became a free person and I have the possibility to dance everywhere if somebody wants to see me and invites me. When we talked before, this was just beginning, New York, Royal [Ballet] and Denmark. It was really my first freedom like this. But after that it continued like non-stop, and I was happy to dance in all the big companies in the world—I learned something from them and I tried to show something for them. And my repertory really looks incredible when you see it. I cannot even name for you everything, because it's more than a hundred ballets and versions. We were locked before, you even could not think and dream about 'Could I do this?' so it came like an explosion for me. And I never had a place where I never came back. I always was welcomed back.

A lot of people would love to do this but they cannot do it. Because...it's not easy. First, traveling, and after two days you need to recover and dance. You need to learn new things, because each production is a little bit different. This is stressful and this is difficult. And another point, not a lot of people are invited to have this opportunity, we can count the few people—it's not so many. And what was very good for me, I always went back to the Bolshoi and worked with Raisa [Struchkova] again. I never was totally out during the year—I was not a person who was just traveling around the world without a home or without a theatre. People who don't have a place to go back and work and make herself...we call this in Russia "clean yourself again"...it's really dangerous and difficult. So it was my choice, I never left the Bolshoi even when I had a difficult situation there, because this is important, to have your home.

Of course, a really big pleasure is to play different roles, and also to meet the great people around the world. We always say if you meet great people and you become friends with these people, as much great people around you, as much rich you are. You understand? My translation is not so good. And I'm so thankful now, because now everybody is with me, everybody comes to Georgia. They respect me, they know what I'm talking about, even about money. Any time I have any question, they are always ready to help and to call me or ask what I need. Now everything I was doing in the world during this period comes back to me. And I'm so thankful for all of them, because...People don't know the company because it had no name for so many years, people didn't even hear of it before.

I think somebody counted my ballets, and my last performance, *Marguerite and Armand*, was 102 or something. That includes all the versions, like I have done seven versions of *Swan Lake* or four versions of *Don Q*. The hard and funny part, when I have a short time to learn some version and the music is the same that I know always, it's so difficult for me to switch. Sometimes it is confusing and it makes me more nervous. If I have new roles to play, like *Manon* with the Royal Ballet...I cannot do it in two days, so I will spend more time to learn and perform. And if the ballet is with partners, you need to be with the partners. Always this kind of ballet needs more preparation.

Video helps a lot, specially because before, you had a coach, you had a teacher who was spending a lot of time with you in the studio. Now everything is hard and difficult—you don't have enough time in the studio or with the person you want. Of course the company always make it as good as possible for a guest ballerina, but people are needed in other places, other rehearsals. It's just 24 hours in the day, we cannot stretch these hours. And always I have this feeling like I want one and a half day more, always.

I prefer to learn the steps in the video and then work with somebody who knows this role and who can coach it for details. This is important, because there are small questions you want to ask about a lot of things, things that make a difference. If I'm dancing something new, I love to watch how several people do the same role, and then I have a little bit more picture of the interpretation of different people and what is right or what is not totally as they like it. At the same time, I start to think how I need to look myself. I remember, when I was in the Royal Ballet, watching the Firebird of Margot Fonteyn on the video. Of course Margot was not jumping like young girls now, but I didn't care, because her character was absolutely great. Small details, how the eyes are looking, where the eyes are looking, how she moves the arms and head. And then, when we worked with Monica Mason I understood much more.

You know, when I'm dancing in New York I don't change any of my style, because I'm dancing there classical—at ABT [American Ballet Theatre], this is my own style. But if we're talking about Denmark, definitely I must change, because the Danish style is different, and I needed to learn it. This is important, to catch their style and do what they're thinking and what they want and *how* they want it—then it's right. You cannot go to Denmark and say, "You know what? I don't want to do Bournonville like this." They know how it should be and how it should look. This is why I spent so much time in Denmark. It was my choice to go there and learn *La Sylphide* and dance all Bournonville's ballets. I wanted to learn, and after this, when I was dancing *La Sylphide* in the Bolshoi, I did what *they* taught me in Denmark, not how [Oleg] Vinogradov teaches them to dance Bournonville. I did my Danish *La Sylphide*, and the others...were different from my vision. I cannot say they were dancing bad—they were dancing good but different, and for me it was not quite correct.

I love to have somebody who will look at me and just say what is good and what is not and criticize. I need it all the time, even now when I coach [others] myself. So I'm so happy that I have Irina Kolpakova at ABT. We have worked like 15 years together, she's with me there all the time, and now I have invited her to come to Georgia—she's my last greatest person, I think. And also in Tbilisi I have two persons helping me: Maya Zurashvili, she was a ballerina, and Irina Jandieri, also she was a ballerina in the Tbilisi [State] Theatre. Every day Maya gives classes to me, and some rehearsals I'm sharing with them, some ballets with this person, some ballets with this other person.

Even when I was with Alexei [Fadeyechev] without Raisa, we helped each other. He helps me a lot now too, he comes to Georgia, and he's teaching me and correcting me. Of course I have some feeling myself about if I do this wrong, but when you have a person who says, "Yes, you're right, it does not look good"...we need this always. This is why ballet is so difficult, because it's not enough if you once do good. It does not stay all the time. You need *every day* to be careful and do good. You know? It's body, it's technical, it's emotional, everything works together if you're training well and you continue to do this every day, every day, every day. If you do it once and then you say, "I have done everything, it's all very nice," the next day it will be totally different and worse and possibly wrong. Of course you go to class to keep your body and your technique in good shape. It reminds yourself and your body to be correct, you need to *work* every day to correct. People sometimes say, "Nina, why do you need to work so hard? You already dance very beautifully and you are a big ballerina." But everything happens *because* I work so hard.

Even now I'm taping myself and watching again. I love to tape rehearsal, not just performance, to check my mistakes. Then I film my dress rehearsal, correct my mistakes, and then I tape my first performance. And technically, I don't cut down anything so far. I don't make it small, I cannot take out some jumps or turns because I'm old...no, nothing, ever. So I continue to do technique like I did before and I should do it, because if I go onstage and dance, I want to be as good as possible. This does not come like I'm sitting on a bench and then I get up and dance, of course not. People say, "Oh, because you have talent." I understood I have talent, from my parents, from...I don't know...God, from my teachers... Of course I have good schooling, everything. But without work for yourself and without discipline, it doesn't happen and it doesn't stay so long.

Now I cannot have one student like Raisa had me because I'm directing, so all the dancers are mine, all are my children, and I love them so much so I try to help all of them. One day when I've decided to stop directing, maybe I can take one young person and just grow them...I would *love* to do this. But so far I have to split my time with all of them. Not just principals—I was never in the corps, so I don't know the secrets of the corps, the eyes and all, but sometimes I look at the corps because it's also my job to watch them. I am learning how I need to look 'round and check everything together—crab eyes, I call it. Tatiana Terekhova... She's a former Kirov ballerina, a great ballerina, she told me, "I try to learn how to see everybody," and I said, "How is it possible?" She said, "Trust me, it's practice." So now I try to really watch everything onstage. And because I have different thoughts and I'm longtime onstage, of course everything that's onstage I control now.

You know, frankly say, it was not my future to direct the company in Georgia, I didn't think about this. I was active ballerina,

I was continuing to dance everywhere, in ABT and the Bolshoi and my tours around. And I thought maybe when I stop dancing I can teach somewhere, I don't know where, but I would love to do this. I know this because when I was at the Bolshoi, sometimes our teacher, Marina [Semyonova], did not come, so they asked me to teach class. And also some dancers asked me to help them to work, and just a little bit I was coaching them. It comes naturally—I see something goes wrong and I say, "You know what? You need to do this," and when they become better, it makes me happy. So I know I like to do this.

But to direct the company, it happened really quickly and without my plan and without my thinking. I was not dreaming to do this at all. It's just that the president of Georgia [Mikheil Saakashvili] called me when he became president and said he wanted to talk with me about this. When I went in Tbilisi [that] August, just on holiday to visit my family, I had a talk with the president. He said, "We need you in Georgia very much. What can we do to have you here to be artistic director of the company, because we need to build again the company and bring back the name of our theatre." So I said, "I cannot say to you I will be good or not, because how do I know? I have never been any other place to direct." I said, "Let me try, but if I try I need..." this and this and this. And especially there was talk about money. And he said, "We will do everything. We give you money for salary and we give you money, separate, for staging ballets." And everything we staged this last three, four years—and we have done 30 ballets—everything was paid by the government.

The condition of the company when I came here was not good. But I don't blame people, because it was really a bad situation in Georgia, the last 15 years especially. There was no money, nobody was taking care about art. And everybody tried to leave to dance; somebody was in Turkey, somebody was in Macedonia, somebody was in a lot of places. But somehow the company still was working, even one performance in the month or in three months, somehow they survived—I think they're all heroes. Without money, without water, without light, without heat, without anything, anyway these people came to the class, and nobody said, "Why do you not pay me?" because they love this job. They continued to come, even by feet—I mean, because they didn't have money to come by bus and car, they came by walking, like an hour walking, to take class and walk back again.

They had a salary officially but they were not paid; there was no money to pay for them. So it was really hard.

Of course something was happening there—I cannot say nothing was happening. [Georgi] Aleksidze, the director before me, was staging his one-act ballets, and he was famous in Russia, so he was staging other places. But nothing was really big, because it was impossible to do something big. And you cannot keep a company if you don't have anything to give the dancers. If they want it, they come; if they don't want it, they don't come—it was like a hobby. People went away and people stayed—both have happened. Somebody who can go out, they go out; somebody who cannot, they still continue to come and take class and keep this theatre. And always myself and…Irma Nioradze and Igor Zelensky or somebody was coming like once or two times during this period. I tried to dance there every year, just to help the company to have a little money for salary or something.

So when I talked with the president, he said "We need you desperately in Georgia. Please. We don't know anybody who can do this better than you. So you need to come back and help us. It's time. I came to help my country and I need people around me like you." And I was sitting there thinking, 'My god, how I can say no to this young man?' If you knew which kind of situation we had in Georgia four years ago, and he really wanted to do everything best. I think it would have been so difficult for me to say, "You know what we should do? Let's make Georgia beautiful and healthy, and then maybe I can think about…" No. I couldn't say this. I said, "OK, let me try. If it works, I promise you after three years I can show you results."

The president said, "I want to announce this myself. Tomorrow. Everybody will be onstage." When I went there he presented myself and two others, just speaking to the company: "This will be the new artistic director, the new chief conductor and the director of the theatre." And I told them, "All of you know me as a ballerina, and all of you like me. So now that I become your boss, maybe you will hate me but you need to follow me, at least in this period."

I had a month, maybe less, to decide, and before I said yes, of course I talked with a lot of people, like Frank Andersen, who was the longtime artistic director with the Royal Ballet Danish. I talked with Kevin [McKenzie, artistic director of ABT] and with Alexei, for their thinking. They're my friends, we have really good relationships, and they said, "Don't worry, we can help you," and they gave me an idea of how I need to communicate with people. It was difficult, but my best friend, Alexei Fadeyechev, who was once artistic director of the Bolshoi, was very much with me at the beginning; he helped me put the company together, and his wife, Tatiana Rastorgueva, was working with the corps and soloist girls very hard. Amazing—the first two months, three of us from the Bolshoi were working there, and of course all the staff that I got from Tbilisi.

The company needed everything. Of course, first I started to pay salary, because they have families and they know if they have a salary they can survive. Second was discipline, discipline, because in the ballet discipline has the first place. You cannot come late, you cannot say, "Oh, today I feel bad, I cannot come to dance the performance." Discipline. I was really strong for that, because life and democracy is what we have now, and people understand democracy is like you don't have to do anything. But democracy is not like that: democracy...you can argue, you can talk, but democracy's not anarchy, not anything goes or without discipline or without law. Especially in our country, in Soviet countries, they understand democracy like, "Oh, we can do anything." But in democracy countries, like America and Japan, you *cannot* do anything, you need to follow rules. Dancers too, of course, everybody. Before, everybody was afraid and they followed rules, but now the young dancers can say, "You cannot talk to me like this." Before, if you were young, how impossible to say these words with the director or a teacher. You could not, and it was stupid to do it. So now, specially in my job...Not everybody's clever, not everybody has discipline inside, so you need to show them and give direction—then it works.

I think we were the last generation...or maybe after us, like five years younger, was the last generation who was much more disciplined and more inside of the job. Now it's hard in a lot of ways, because...Everywhere in the world, in Russia too, ballet is not so prestigious and not making so much money like the person who is a secretary or something. Before, parents give children the schooling because, "Oh my god, they will be famous, they will live better, they will have more money, they can see the world." Now, you're a secretary, you're making more money and you can go out and see the world, and you don't need to work so hard. I cannot say the dancers are not working hard now in Georgia. But their style of life, maybe it's quick, and everything comes quickly.

So the company needed discipline, and also repertory and quality of classes and quality of coaches, everything. For the first two months they were working without salary. When I took the job, it was like the middle of September, and we had money for November. So I said to them, "We don't have money now, I cannot pay you. You can be free and we can start in November, and then we can have the first performance in January. But if we start working now, we can have performances in November and also salary in November." And everybody said, "We're ready to work now," and all of them were working immediately to make a program in November, with a première. It was the first time for a mixed bill program, and we sold all the tickets and even put extra ones, because it was really a success.

You know what they needed from me? I show them my character and I try to be an example for them, because each company has stressful situations, not enough time, we cannot do this, costume is not ready or something, something, something. So you always need to find something positive in this moment, because if everybody will be crazy, nothing happens. So I try to teach them you don't need to be screaming, everything can be done normally. Also, if they have a problem, not just about ballet but family or something, they always can come and talk with me, and we can find a way to help them. And they respect me, and what we did together...I don't know any other place in the world that can do this much work, because they follow me without any question.

The company is a hundred dancers—I have a hundred and forty with the administration and everybody—and we have now 30 ballets. In the beginning I started to do classical ballets, because if you're a classical company you cannot be without them. You need them for training dancers, so it's necessary to have Russian classics like *Swan Lake, Giselle, Don Q, Nutcracker*. We love to perform these, for us it's not old-fashioned. In my company they're fighting each other to play classical ballets, and even in the Bolshoi, we always want to dance even more classical ballets. Generally, people love to be in the classics, because they are much more difficult to dance, and if you are good in a classical ballet you show your level.

It's interesting why these ballets are still alive—because they're great. And each person who stages them gives a new look. The classical ballets I have, specially *Don Q*, *Swan Lake* and *Giselle*, these are Alexei Fadeyechev productions, and Alexei made a little pas de six inside *Giselle* that is more dancing and more interesting to watch. So we try to give a new look but keep the really genius dancing. And the corps does beautifully—my god, you don't want to see anything else. I try to teach it to make the corps important, this is really important for me. The corps is not like machinery people, they're not circus, they're not Chinese opera, they're live people and they need to dance the corps' dances live. People write about our corps de ballet in *Giselle*, that their movement is live and soft and really beautiful.

The most difficult thing in the world is to make their moving and acting right. They learn the steps, but to put the steps together with emotion and with movement, it's a little bit more difficult now, in this period. I specially take care of this and I'm specially more strong with this than with the technical, but technical should also be done well. And I tell you, Georgian people are born artistic, they're naturally artistic people. So there's just a need to show them how they need to bring this out, and it's my job to try to make sure this happens onstage.

We continue to invite choreographers to stage for us specially; we have Stanton Welch, Trey McIntyre, we have nine ballets of Balanchine, and these mixed programs are very successful, even in Georgia where…You need to understand, not a lot of people live in Tblisi and we don't have so many tourists. So it's not like people come to see our opera house like at Covent Garden because they want to say, "I went to see Covent Garden." Nearly the same audience comes to watch every performance, and for the last three years we improved the ticket sales at home every year. And you know how much the company changed? In one year they started learning different styles and they started learning much quicker. Before, it was so difficult to learn something else, because they never did it and never saw it.

We do three programs of Balanchine, and Balanchine is fantastic training for the company, perfect, wonderful, because you start thinking differently about classical ballet. Balanchine is classical ballet now, even his neoclassical things, and he gives the idea that the classical ballet vocabulary is much more than you think about in Petipa's ballets. All the ballets of Balanchine…it's like steps working and movements working and counting differently and timing differently—it really helps a dancer to grow.

My taste now is a little bit different because I've seen a lot of things, and now maybe I like Stravinsky more than the audience, who is not always happy to see it so far. But what is interesting, every time we perform Balanchine's Stravinsky, *Duo Concertant* or *Apollo*, or we have another something with difficult music, the audiences go crazy, they like it so much. They appreciate this great music that they did not know before—I'm talking about Georgia. I do repertory, of course, for the company, to grow them and to see what they can do better, and I do it for the audience, because I grow my audience also. So far I try to keep the prices low, because I want to make this for everybody. For every Sunday they can buy like an...*abonnement*, subscription, and this is priced a little bit lower. This is at three o'clock in the afternoon, so children can come, even I perform for them. The program is not specially for children—we have everything that we perform during the year, so they see serious ballets, Balanchine, all our new things, everything, and it gives me an absolutely fantastic feeling when I see, every time, every Sunday, it's sold out. And I know after five years these children come back to me as audience. All of them already know the names of the dancers...I see children 12 years old, they start talking, "Oh, did you see last week...?"

I'm so happy to see now in Georgia the children and also students and a young generation comes. Even in Japan—before, it was just woman watching the stage, now a young man comes to watch. This winter we had like a one-month tour in the United States and we performed *Giselle* in student cities, in the university theatres there. And I thought, 'My god, for students it will be so boring to see this kind of ballet. Will they understand it?' Then I had a lecture with them after the performance and I asked them, "What do you feel? Is it boring, somebody in a long dress walking around and doing this pantomime?" And they said, "Absolutely not," because they understood that this is theatre, that it's a story that can happen now and they were just watching how it was in a different century. For me it was very interesting, because this is exactly what we want to show. This is our feeling, our soul, our story that we show today. Even though we play it like people of other centuries, it's still true. And they said they understood everything and they didn't need any interpretation, so if it's done well and it is beautiful, it's not boring. All people love to see big classical ballet, three acts, everywhere in the world the same. You see a lot of people go to modern dance, but somehow in big houses, classical ballet sells tickets.

You know, I'm directing the school too. I have 200 children, maybe even more now, from six to eighteen years. But it's a problem: I don't have many boys. We have the Georgian classical ballet school, it's a government school, with Vaganova's system of teaching. I did change something there a little bit, just to put more, not less. I put more drama lessons for the students, not ballet-way drama but real drama lessons, so my dancers can talk and act more. And also I put t'ai chi lessons, which help me—I did this already for 30 years and I see the wonderful results.

One thing that I do now differently also: for four years' preparation, I take people from six years old until ten. After ten years old, we already see who is best to put into the classical ballets. So, at ten years old we take them in the ballet school, and after three years, when they are 13 years or 14 years old, I just place them. If somebody is good and perfect for ballet, I keep them for ballet. If bodies change or the shape is not so good, we move them to character dance, and they continue to learn acting and ballet and modern dance and everything. We give them the possibility to stay in our school. We have our teachers, Georgian...Georgian-Russian... Georgian citizen teachers. I'm not teaching but I watch classes and I see the children; every Monday I spend time at the school and every month I have to watch classes.

Also, every year we have school performances. We have repertory like *Paquita, Cinderella, Chopiniana, La Sylphide*, specially for children, so the children can perform in the opera house. And also we make ballets for them, so this year the new ballet is *Midsummer Night's Dream* from our ballet master and choreographer, Nukri Magalashvili, a Georgian.

I am so lucky to have people around me all my years like my school teacher Natalia Zolotova and Raisa Struchkova and Semyonova. Now I respect them more because now I understand how many things they taught me and how many things they put in my head. So now I try to share this with my [Georgian] teachers. They are all very professional, they are educated in Moscow or St. Petersburg or somewhere. So I try to explain to them what I want them to teach to the students in *this* moment. I point them to what I see good around the world or what I see not, and we work together.

I really miss these big people, like Raisa. I can remember all the corrections like a book. I always use them and I say, "Like

Raisa..." or "Like Natalia told me." When we were in the school Natalia taught us...not only taught us but taught us how to teach. She tried to teach us to see first what is wrong and second what you need to do to correct it. To have open eyes always—if you see something good, you try to do it yourself, and if you see something wrong, you write in your head, 'I must be careful not to do that.' I didn't learn this by a book—I learned this from her. And now I'm shocked by how much I know.

Very few people in the world now really know and understand classical ballet. All the boys are doing *Don Q* everywhere, but you can't do *Don Q* arms in *Sleeping Beauty*, you cannot. The style is the style. You must see the difference of time, style and especially place, if it's Spain for *Don Q* or Hungary for *Raymonda*. Nikolai Fadeyechev and his son, Alexei, know this. Kolpakova, Semyonova, Tatiana Terekhova—a great coach—know these differences and *care* about them.

What is interesting between the great teacher and the good teacher is the small things, because they care even about where the eye is looking.

I try to dance *Giselle* like Raisa coached me, and I try to remember all the small details that she put in my head when I was little. But of course my Giselle is different now than before, because I'm dancing more and a lot of else and because something comes of my own, my feeling, which I think improved it. A lot of things come inside, and you want to take them out and show the audience. I'm not doing anything special—it comes naturally because I'm now longtime on stage. But what is really interesting, a few weeks ago I was dancing *Giselle* in New York, and some famous people of influence and critics told me, "Nina, you're dancing *Giselle* like we remember *Giselle* old period with the great ballerinas, especially the first act." Very few people now play *Giselle* first act like it was in Ulanova's period, Struchkova's period. They were very strong and strict about the first act. Now people are thinking that if the character is more usual, more normal, more in *this* modern time, it will be more interesting for the audience, and they're losing the magic that is between the first and second act. So I try to keep all they taught me and be myself, I mean, be my Giselle like I feel it. Suzanne [Farrell] taught me *Mozartiana* and then she told me, "That's all I can show you. Now you finish it—put yourself in it. That's what Balanchine told me to do, so I'm telling you the same thing."

Not because you change something in your performance when you dance other things, but these other things give you something else that maybe you can use or put into this performance. I cannot say how and what, but it's like...When you read a lot of books, you don't start talking differently. You talk the same, but your knowledge and your mind are much more than before the books, right? It's like inside of you. It's the same feeling in the ballet. As much you dance, as much you know; as much you know, as much you use. Everything goes in and then you explode, it comes out.

I always go onstage and dance like I'm dancing for the last time. I must think like this, because who knows what will happen tomorrow. Why save for then? And Raisa told me, "Don't forget—it doesn't matter how you feel yourself. Whether it's one or two or five or twenty, you have to dance for the audience. You have to dance for the person there for the first time or last time. Someone will follow you every second, watching." This makes the difference between a big artist and others.

I'm still ABT's ballerina, but next season will be my last. And the Bolshoi...officially I did not...say goodbye or something, no. They invite me to dance, several times, but I cannot make it because of my schedule. So who knows. If I continue to dance and they want to invite me, I will dance with big pleasure. It's a new, different company now. I have, of course, people I know there, my partners, my colleagues, but it has a young generation now, and the style...I think they've changed a little bit, they've become more like a modern company...not modern, I cannot say modern, more like a western company. They have any kind of ballets now, a lot of modern ballets, they have Twyla Tharp, and they enjoy to do this. But I think it's good, it should be like this; you cannot keep a company to do just Russian classics. You need to move a company. But. I'm worrying...If you see my classical ballets in Georgia, I'm very strong, maybe even a little bit too strong, for taste. I love to keep Russian taste what it was and what my teachers taught me. Because I hate it, especially in the classical ballets, when the taste of dance goes like *kick* legs up and do faces and too much this and too much that. I like a big extension, of course, beautiful, but what makes me sad about the Kirov Ballet and the Bolshoi, they start doing this now all the time, whether you need it or you don't need it.

When I see new modern choreography, I just see splits and splits and splits; sometimes I say, "My god, can I see one choreographer who doesn't use a split at all and makes a beautiful ballet and good choreography?" In some modern ballets and Balanchine ballets it's necessary, like *Rubies* or something, but not in the classical ballets. It breaks the line, it breaks the story, it is not about legs up. I don't have this extension, but people come to see my performance, not my triple pirouettes—it's about art. I'm so careful about this in my company. You know, there is an old saying: "In our time, our dogs were barking differently." I talked with Altynai [Asylmuratova] about this—she now runs the [Vaganova] school—and she said, "I tell the dancers not to do these extensions, and they say, 'But if we don't do this at auditions, we don't get the jobs.' So what can I do?"

I have my own audience still everywhere. They follow me, they continue to come, they even become old a little bit. But frankly say, the last four years I'm not traveling a lot. I was 42 when I had my baby. I was so happy to have a child, at my age specially, and I have Elena. But there are several reasons why I have not stopped dancing. First, I don't want Elena to be the reason, like *she* stopped me. Even more, maybe I can say first place...When I took this job, my Raisa Struchkova was alive, and she was like my mother, I call her my Russian mother, so I took care of her all this last period [of her life]. She was so upset because, she said, "If you take this job, you will stop dancing. Don't stop dancing, because you are in such good shape." I said, "Raisa, I will continue to dance, but I will at the same time direct the company." And she told me, "Please, promise me not to stop dancing yet." So I said, "But if I have a baby?" She said, "No, there's no time for a baby now." "But if it happens?" She said, "So what. It doesn't matter. You can come back."

It was the last talk we had about ballet, and then she became really sick and more sick. So then I tried to just talk with her about what I'm doing in Georgia, and she said, "It's wonderful, but don't stop dancing." She kept saying this, very slow, and her mind was 'til the end very clear. So I said to myself inside—at that time I was not pregnant—'Even if I have a baby, I need to do everything to come back, for Raisa.'

I was two years out. It was so difficult, so difficult, to come back, but I'm totally crazy, so my first performance was *Swan Lake*, after two years, and then *Don Q*. And I said, "If I am dancing this kind of ballet, then I'm really in shape and I can continue to do it." Then everything else, I just enjoy. There was one role

I always wanted to do, Ashton's *Marguerite and Armand*. It was my longtime dream, and in May we made a full Ashton's ballet evening in Tbilisi, and I performed this ballet. Nobody has this except the Royal Ballet—just we have this one. Oh, there is a lot more that I want to do, because I'm really back on my level. I think I'm also a comedy artist but not so many people see me as that, and I love to do new works made for me. I have so much inside that I can show for the audience. And it's funny, but I'm still thinking I never danced my best ballet yet. I don't know what it will be, but somehow I feel no choreographer used my... everything so far. Who knows, maybe it will never happen, and I will stop dancing still with this feeling. I hope it happens. I need to rush a little bit.

And one last reason why I continue to dance: because I'm directing the company and the company needs my support. To take the company away, to the United States or Japan or even here in Edinburgh, they need a name to go on a tour, because a name sells tickets. It was like on my shoulders: I need to show this company, and without me it will be nearly impossible, frankly say, because producers always ask, "Nina, are you dancing? If you dance, yes. If not, no dice." So far *I* take *them*, because I am with them, I am dancing. Now when people see my dancers and slowly I make the name of the company, it will be much easier for me. Now people enjoy the company and they understand the level of the company, it's not like "Nina Ananiashvili with somebody." It's like, "The Georgian State Ballet level is *something*." Even in the United States, they say, "The Georgian company...Its standard can make competition for the Bolshoi and the Kirov." We already went two times to Japan and we have plans to go again to Japan and to the Spoleto Festival in the United States. Here in the Edinburgh Festival...We are so happy—this [Playhouse] is the biggest theatre, like three thousand people, and it was packed for five performances, really amazing. Edinburgh was very important for me because a lot of people saw the company, we have good reviews here, and it was Europe. So now I look forward to having more invitations from Europe.

What is very interesting and a most difficult thing: to find a face for the company. Because now, everybody has everything, right? Before, the Russian classics were just in Russia. *Bayadère*, *Raymonda*, *Corsaire*...these ballets were just Russian ballets. They never happened in America, and people were interested to see these danced by Russians. Now everybody has *Bayadère, Raymonda*, everything. It's so difficult to have something exclusive. So I love to have new repertory. We revived Vakhtang Chabukiani's *Laurencia*, and nobody else has it. Even the one-act ballets, like *Sagalobeli* [by Yuri Possokhov], that's ours, Georgian—just *we* do this. Of course, I am Georgian but I am a Russian ballerina, I cannot do anything different. So we have Russian training. But what I love to see and what now I can see is that my company has a different face for everything. By style I can say we have Russian style. But by face...I'm happy that I found my company's face, and it is different.

It's a difficult, terrible situation now, when we are here, because all our families are there [in Georgia], we don't know what's going on, and dancers were crying before the performance because they were really nervous and upset. And it was so hard for me, because I have my family there also that I worry about and a husband inside this problem [in the government], and at the same time I have 80 people here and I need to say to them, "Dance. We cannot cancel the performance." You know what people say to me here in Edinburgh? I'm so proud of this. People in the audience stopped me and said, "Can you go to talk with the dancers?" I said yes—I don't say who I am. "Please tell them, you are ambassadors of your country. And we appreciate it, and we love your art. Thank you so much for dancing and not canceling," and a lot of compliments and wonderful words. So it's *our* country's problem, it's *our* hearts breaking, but they're supporting us this way, all of them who come to watch our performance.

This is for our country, what we did here now, and I think our people in Georgia appreciated this. And definitely they did here, everybody, each person. Even in the street—you won't believe it—they see ballet dancers coming, they stop you—the girls told me this—"You are from the Georgia State Ballet? We are with you," and they start again to say compliments. Russian actors came yesterday to our performance with a big basket of flowers to give to our people. There was writing here, on the back of the shirt, "Russian," especially to show they are Russian and they respect us. It doesn't matter what nationality you are. This war is not about people—this is about politics that should be stopped, it is terrible.

I tell you one thing. My grandma, when she was alive...She was an amazing person and she had seen revolution...like in '37, when everybody was in the gulag and killed. Then she lived with war, the Second World War. Then she saw '57, when it was a terrible situation again in Georgia, when the Russians came and put all the students in prison because we wanted our language...She saw this, she saw that, all her life, she was even in the war herself because she was a doctor. And she always told me, "Even in those difficult times when we had war, we always needed artists, we always needed people who come and play for us. We understood it was not the time for singing, but this gave us energy to continue, energy to feel we're still alive, energy to feel like we can grow back, we can live more. If it's not us, we do this for our next generation."

So the next plan is continue to work. The next plan is for me to build a new school in Tbilisi, a new building with a theatre and everything—it will be the best school in the world. And I promise, in a few years...Now I take myself and the company everywhere. But for the future I want to split my dancers...There will be Georgian ballerinas in each company in the world.

Edinburgh
August 2008

Index